CW00392219

## Disclaimer

The information provided in this book is for educational purposes only and should not be construed as financial or investment advice. Options trading involve risks, and past performance does not guarantee future results. The author and publisher are not liable for any financial losses incurred by readers based on the information provided in this book. Always consult with a qualified financial advisor before making any investment decisions.

# Acknowledgement

I am deeply grateful and indebted to many people who have supported me throughout my journey in writing this book. Their unwavering love, encouragement, and belief in me have been the driving force behind this endeavor. I would like to express my heartfelt gratitude to:

Late Shri Bhabhooti Ram Gautam: My beloved father, whose wisdom, guidance, and unwavering support have shaped me into the person I am today. Though he is no longer with us, his teachings and values continue to inspire me every day.

Mrs. Susheela Devi: My loving mother, whose nurturing presence has been a constant source of strength and motivation. Her boundless love and sacrifices have been instrumental in making this dream a reality.

Family and Kids: To all my family members, including my dear spouse, siblings, and relatives, who have stood by my side throughout this writing journey, offering encouragement, understanding, and invaluable feedback.

Lastly, my wonderful kids, who have been the light of my life. Your innocence and unconditional love have kept me grounded and focused, reminding me of the importance of this book's legacy.

I dedicate this book to the memory of my late father, with a heart full of love and gratitude. His blessings have been the guiding light that led me through every step of this writing process.

Thank you all for being a part of my life and for supporting me in pursuing my passion for sharing knowledge and insights about options trading in the Indian market. Your presence in my life is an invaluable gift, and I am blessed to have each one of you.

With love and gratitude,

Shambhu Nath Gautam

## Preface

Welcome to "Mastering Options Trading in the Indian Market." This book is a comprehensive guide designed to equip you with the knowledge, skills, and strategies necessary to navigate the fascinating world of options trading in the Indian financial landscape. Whether you are a novice investor seeking to understand the basics or an experienced trader aiming to enhance your proficiency, this book is here to empower you.

Options trading, a dynamic and versatile financial instrument, has gained significant popularity in recent years. It offers traders the potential to capitalize on market movements, manage risks, and generate substantial returns, all within a defined risk framework. However, delving into options trading can be daunting without a clear understanding of its nuances, unique jargon, and underlying principles.

The inspiration to pen this book emerged from my passion for finance and a desire to share knowledge that can empower others in their financial journey. I have spent years exploring and honing my expertise in options trading, and through this book, I aim to demystify this intricate subject, making it accessible to readers from all walks of life.

In "Mastering Options Trading in the Indian Market," you will embark on a step-by-step journey, starting with the fundamentals of options and gradually advancing to more complex strategies. We will explore the various option types, delve into the intricacies of options pricing, and discuss how to effectively use options in both bullish and bearish market scenarios.

Moreover, I have included real-world examples, case studies, and practical tips to enhance your understanding and provide you with the tools needed to make informed decisions. While this book primarily focuses on the Indian financial markets, the concepts and principles can be applied to options trading in other global markets as well.

I must emphasize that options trading involves risks and should not be undertaken lightly. Throughout the book, I will emphasize risk management strategies and the importance of developing a disciplined approach to trading.

My sincere hope is that "Mastering Options Trading in the Indian Market" serves as a valuable resource in your financial education and helps you develop a solid foundation in options trading. May this knowledge empower you to make well-informed decisions, navigate the markets with confidence, and achieve your financial goals?

Happy reading and successful trading!

Shambhu Nath Gautam

## Table of Contents

**Chapter 1: Introduction to Options Trading**                    **(12-22)**

1.1    Understanding Options                                          12
1.1.1    What Are Options?                                           12
1.1.2    Call and Put Options                                        14
1.1.3    Option Pricing and Valuation                                16
1.1.4    Option Greeks                                               16

1.2 Option Trading Mechanics in Indian Markets                       18

1.3 Importance of Options Trading Strategies                         19

1.4 Risks and Rewards of Options Trading                             21

**Chapter 2: Getting Started with Options Trading**               **(23-29)**

2.1 Setting/Opening up a Trading Account                             23

2.2 Option Symbols and Expiration Dates                              23

2.3 Option Chains and Quotes                                         25

2.4 Placing Option Trades                                            25

2.5 Understanding Trading Platforms and Tools                        27

2.6 Commonly Used Option Trading Terms                               28

**Chapter 3: Option Strategies for Beginners**                    **(30-36)**

3.1 Buying Call Options                                              30

3.2 Buying Put Options                                               30

3.3 Covered Call Strategy                                            31

3.4 Protective Put Strategy                                          31

3.5 The Bull Call Spread                                             32

3.6 The Bear Put Spread                                              33

3.7 Bullish and Bearish Vertical Spreads                             33

3.8 Collars and Risk Management                                      35

**Chapter 4: Advanced Option Trading Strategies**                 **(37-47)**

4.1 Long Straddle Strategy                                           37

4.2 Long Strangle Strategy                                           37

4.3 Iron Condors and Iron Butterflies                                38

4.4 Calendar Spread Strategy    40

4.5 Diagonal Spreads    40

4.6 Ratio Spreads    41

4.7 Synthetic Positions    43

4.8 Strategies for Market Volatility    44

4.8.1 Dealing with High Volatility in the Market    44

4.8.2 Volatility-Based Options Trading Strategies    44

4.8.3 Hedging Techniques during Market Turmoil    44

4.9 Options Trading for Income Generation    45

4.9.1 Income-Generating Strategies with Options    45

4.9.2 Covered Calls and Cash-Secured Puts for Income    45

4.9.3 Dividend Arbitrage with Options    46

**Chapter 5: Options Trading with Indian Shares**    **(48-54)**

5.1 Analyzing Indian Stocks for Options Trading    48

5.2 Best Practices for Option Trading with Indian Shares    50

5.3 Case Studies with Indian Share Options    53

**Chapter 6: Options Trading with Nifty**    **(55-58)**

6.1 Nifty Options: An Overview    55

6.2 Trading Nifty Call and Put Options    55

6.3 Hedging with Nifty Options    56

6.4 Case Studies with Nifty Options    56

**Chapter 7: Options Trading with Bank Nifty**    **(59-62**

7.1 Bank Nifty Options: An Introduction    59

7.2 Strategies for Trading Bank Nifty Options    60

7.3 Leveraging Bank Nifty Options for Income Generation    60

7.4 Case Studies with Bank Nifty Options    61

**Chapter 8: Technical Analysis for Option Trading**    **(63-67)**

8.1 Understanding Charts and Trends    63

8.2 Support and Resistance Levels      64

8.3 Moving Averages and Oscillators      64

8.4 Chart Patterns and Candlestick Analysis      65

8.5 Using Technical Indicators with Options      66

**Chapter 9: Fundamental Analysis for Option Trading**      **(68-71)**

9.1 Economic Indicators and Market News      68

9.2 Earnings Reports and Company Analysis      68

9.3 Event-driven Trading with Options      69

9.4 Sector Analysis and ETF Options      70

9.5 Interpreting Options Sentiment      70

**Chapter 10: Risk Management and Position Sizing**      **(72-75)**

10.1 Setting Risk Tolerance      72

10.2 Diversification and Portfolio Allocation      72

10.3 Using Stop Losses, Limit Orders and Trailing Stops      72

10.4 Managing Position Sizes      73

10.5 Managing Margin and Leverage      73

10.6 Hedging and Risk Mitigation      74

**Chapter 11: Psychology of Option Trading**      **(76-89)**

11.1 Emotions and Decision Making      76

11.2 Maintaining Discipline and Patience      78

11.3 Handling Losses and Drawdowns      79

11.4 Developing a Trading Plan      81

11.5 Mindfulness and Mental Well-being      84

11.6 Managing Fear and Greed in Options Trading      86

11.7 Visualization and Goal Setting      87

**Chapter 12: Building a Trading System and Strategy**      **(90-99)**

12.1 Defining Your Trading Style and Goals      90

12.2 Components of a Trading System      91

12.3 Strategy Development and Testing 93

12.4 Optimization and Parameter Selection 95

12.5 System Monitoring and Evaluation 97

**Chapter 13: Backtesting and Paper Trading (100-102)**

13.1 Importance of Backtesting 100

13.2 Creating a Backtesting Plan 100

13.3 Paper Trading Strategies 101

13.4 Analyzing Backtesting Results 101

13.5 Incorporating Backtesting into Your Trading Routine 101

**Chapter 14: Tips for Successful Options Trading in India(103-105)**

14.1 The Importance of Discipline and Patience 103

14.2 Avoiding Common Mistakes in Options Trading 103

14.3 Keeping Up with Market Trends and News 104

14.4 The Role of Emotions in Trading 104

**Chapter 15: The Future of Options Trading in India (106-108)**

15.1 Evolving Market Trends 106

15.2 Technology and Innovation in Options Trading 106

15.3 Global Market Integration and Impact on Indian Options Trading 107

**Chapter 16: Lessons Learned (109-111)**

16.1 Lessons Learned from Failures and Mistakes 109

16.2 Adapting to Changing Market Conditions 109

16.3 Overcoming Challenges in Options Trading 109

**Conclusion (112)**

**Notes (113-114)**

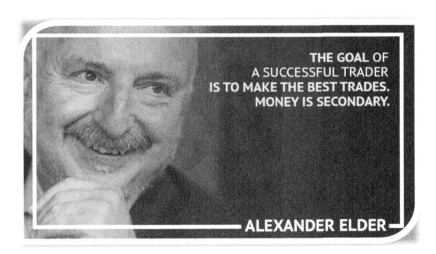

THE GOAL OF
A SUCCESSFUL TRADER
IS TO MAKE THE BEST TRADES.
MONEY IS SECONDARY.

ALEXANDER ELDER

# Introduction

Welcome to the captivating world of options trading in the Indian market! The book you are about to embark upon, "Mastering Options Trading in the Indian Market," is a comprehensive guide that aims to demystify the intricacies of options trading and empower you to become a skilled and confident options trader.

Options, as financial instruments, offer unique opportunities to capitalize on market movements, hedge risks, and potentially achieve impressive returns. They are versatile and can be used in various strategies to suit different market conditions. However, navigating the world of options trading can be challenging without a solid understanding of the underlying principles and strategies involved.

The inspiration for this book stems from my passion for finance and the desire to share knowledge gained through years of experience in trading and investing. I firmly believe that financial literacy is essential for anyone seeking to take control of their financial destiny. With this book, I aim to provide you with a clear and comprehensive understanding of options trading, catering to readers with diverse levels of expertise, whether you are a novice or an experienced trader looking to refine your skills.

In this book, we will start our journey by laying a strong foundation, explaining the fundamental concepts of options trading in simple terms. We will cover topics such as option types, options pricing, and the factors that influence their value. As we progress, we will delve into more sophisticated strategies, exploring bullish, bearish, and neutral market scenarios.

One of the strengths of this book lies in its focus on the Indian financial markets. While options trading is a global phenomenon, the Indian market has its unique characteristics, rules, and dynamics. Understanding the nuances specific to the Indian context will equip you to make well-informed decisions that align with your trading objectives.

To enhance your learning experience, we will use real-world examples, case studies, and practical tips to illustrate the concepts discussed. Moreover, we will emphasize the importance of risk management and cultivating a disciplined approach to options trading.

However, I must emphasize that options trading involves inherent risks, and there are no full proof strategies. The key to successful options trading lies in understanding these risks and employing effective risk management techniques to safeguard your capital.

As you embark on this journey of mastering options trading in the Indian market, I hope that this book serves as a valuable resource in your quest for financial growth and empowerment. May it provide you with the knowledge and tools necessary to navigate the world of options trading with confidence and success?

Here's to your prosperous and fulfilling journey in the world of options trading!

## Chapter 1: Introduction to Options Trading

### 1.1 Understanding Options:

Options are financial contracts that provide the holder with the right, but not the obligation, to buy or sell an underlying asset at a predetermined price (strike price) on or before a specific date (expiration date). These underlying assets can include individual stocks, stock indices like Nifty and Bank Nifty, commodities, currencies, and more. Options offer traders flexibility and the potential for profit in various market conditions.

Option trading in India has a relatively short but eventful history. The concept of options trading, where traders have the right to buy or sell an asset at a predetermined price on or before a specific date, was introduced in India in the early 2000s. The Indian option market was first introduced on June 4, 2001, with the launch of stock options on two leading Indian stock exchanges - the National Stock Exchange of India (NSE) and the Bombay Stock Exchange (BSE). Initially, only a few actively traded stocks were offered as underlying assets for options trading.

### 1.1.1 What Are Options?

Options are financial derivatives whose value is derived from the price movements of an underlying asset. The underlying asset can be a stock, an index (like Nifty or Bank Nifty in the Indian market), a commodity, a currency, or even another derivative instrument. Options give the holder the right, but not the obligation, to buy (call option) or sell (put option) the underlying asset at a predetermined price (strike price) on or before a specified date (expiration date).

To better understand how options derive their value from the underlying asset, let's break down the concept in detail:

Call Option:

A call option gives the holder the right to buy the underlying asset at the strike price on or before the expiration date. Call options are purchased by investors who anticipate that the price of the underlying asset will rise in the future.

When you buy a call option, you pay a premium to the seller of the option. The premium is the cost of holding the right to buy the asset at the specified strike price.

As the price of the underlying asset increases, the call option becomes more valuable. This is because the option holder can purchase the asset at the lower strike price and then sell it in the market at the higher current price, making a profit.

The maximum potential loss for the call option buyer is limited to the premium paid. If the price of the underlying asset does not rise above the strike price by the expiration date, the option may expire worthless, and the buyer loses the premium.

Put Option:

A put option gives the holder the right to sell the underlying asset at the strike price on or before the expiration date. Put options are purchased by investors who expect the price of the underlying asset to decline in the future.

Similar to call options, buying a put option requires paying a premium. This premium represents the cost of having the right to sell the asset at the specified strike price.

As the price of the underlying asset decreases, the put option becomes more valuable. The option holder can buy the asset in the market at the lower current price and then sell it at the higher strike price, making a profit.

The maximum potential loss for the put option buyer is limited to the premium paid. If the price of the underlying asset remains above the strike price by the expiration date, the option may expire worthless, and the buyer loses the premium.

Deriving Option Value from the Underlying Asset:

The value of an option is determined by several factors, including:

Intrinsic Value: The difference between the current price of the underlying asset and the option's strike price. For call options, it is the greater of (current asset price - strike price) or 0. For put options, it is the greater of (strike price - current asset price) or 0.

Time Value: The additional premium paid above the intrinsic value, representing the potential for the option to gain value before expiration. Time value diminishes as the expiration date approaches.

Volatility: Higher volatility in the underlying asset's price leads to higher option premiums, as there is a greater probability of significant price movements.

Interest Rates: Changes in interest rates can also influence option prices, particularly for longer-term options.

The interaction of these factors determines the overall value of the option. Traders use various option pricing models, with the Black-Scholes model being the most common, to calculate the theoretical fair value of an option based on these factors.

Options are derivatives that derive their value from the price movements of the underlying asset. Call options gain value when the asset's price rises, while put options gain value when the asset's price falls. The value of an option is a combination of intrinsic value (if any) and time value, influenced by factors such as volatility and interest rates. Understanding these dynamics is crucial for making informed decisions in options trading in the Indian market.

1.1.2 Call and Put Options:

Call Option: A call option gives the holder the right to buy the underlying asset at the strike price on or before the expiration date. Buyers of call options speculate on the price of the underlying asset rising, and they aim to profit from price increases.

Put Option: A put option gives the holder the right to sell the underlying asset at the strike price on or before the expiration date. Buyers of put options speculate on the price of the underlying asset falling, and they aim to profit from price decreases.

In the context of the Indian market, let's consider some examples using Indian shares, Nifty, and Bank Nifty:

Example 1: Call Option on Indian Share

Suppose you want to buy a call option on Infosys, an Indian IT company. Infosys is currently trading at Rs. 3,000 per share, and you believe the stock price will rise in the next month. You buy a call option with a strike price of Rs. 3,200 and an expiration date one month from now. You pay a premium of Rs. 50 for the option.

Scenario 1: If Infosys's stock price remains below Rs. 3,200 until the expiration date, you may choose not to exercise the option. In this case, your maximum loss will be the premium of Rs. 50.

Scenario 2: If Infosys's stock price rises to Rs. 3,500 by the expiration date, you can exercise the call option and buy Infosys shares at the strike price of Rs. 3,200. Your profit will be Rs. (3,500 - 3,200 - 50) = Rs. 250.

Example 2: Put Option on Nifty

Suppose you want to buy a put option on the Nifty index. The Nifty is currently trading at 15,000 points, and you expect a market downturn in the next two months. You buy a put option with a strike price of 14,500 and an expiration date two months from now. You pay a premium of 200 points for the option.

Scenario 1: If the Nifty index remains above 14,500 until the expiration date, you may choose not to exercise the option. In this case, your maximum loss will be the premium of 200 points.

Scenario 2: If the Nifty index falls to 14,000 by the expiration date, you can exercise the put option and sell the Nifty at the strike price of 14,500. Your profit will be 300 points (14,500 - 14,000 - 200).

Example 3: Call Option on Bank Nifty

Suppose you want to buy a call option on Bank Nifty, which represents the banking sector in India. Bank Nifty is currently trading at 35,000 points, and you expect a bullish trend in the banking sector in the next three months. You buy a call option with a strike price of 36,000 and an expiration date three months from now. You pay a premium of 500 points for the option.

Scenario 1: If Bank Nifty remains below 36,000 until the expiration date, you may choose not to exercise the option. In this case, your maximum loss will be the premium of 500 points.

Scenario 2: If Bank Nifty rises to 38,000 by the expiration date, you can exercise the call option and buy Bank Nifty at the strike price of 36,000. Your profit will be 1,500 points (38,000 - 36,000 - 500).

Please note that these examples are simplified for illustrative purposes and do not take into account factors like option Greeks, transaction costs, and taxes. Options trading involves risks, and it's essential to conduct thorough research, practice with virtual trading, and, if necessary, seek advice from financial professionals before engaging in options trading in the Indian market.

### 1.1.3 Option Pricing and Valuation:

Option pricing is a complex process influenced by several factors:

Current Stock Price: The higher the current stock price concerning the call option's strike price, or the lower concerning the put option's strike price, the higher the option premium.

Strike Price: In relation to the current stock price, the distance between the strike price and the stock price affects the option premium. Options with strike prices closer to the current stock price generally have higher premiums.

Time until Expiration: As the expiration date approaches, the option's time value decreases. Options with more time to expiration tend to have higher premiums.

Market Volatility: Higher market volatility increases the option premium, as it increases the probability of the underlying asset reaching more extreme price levels.

Interest Rates: Changes in interest rates can impact option prices, particularly for options with longer expirations.

### 1.1.4 Option Greeks:

Option Greeks are measures that help traders understand how the option's price is affected by changes in various factors:

Delta: Delta measures the change in an option's price concerning a 1-point change in the underlying asset (in this case, the Indian Rupee, INR). For call options, the delta is positive and typically ranges between 0 and 1. For put options, the delta is negative and ranges between 0 and -1.

If a call option has a delta of 0.6, it means that for every 1-point increase in the INR's value, the call option's price will increase by 0.60 INR.

If a put option has a delta of -0.4, it means that for every 1-point increase in the INR's value, the put option's price will decrease by 0.40 INR.

Example: Consider a call option on Nifty with a delta of 0.7. If the INR appreciates against the US Dollar (USD) by 1 INR, the call option's price will increase by 0.70 INR.

Gamma: Gamma measures the rate of change of an option's delta concerning a 1-point change in the underlying asset's value (INR in this case).

Gamma is highest for at-the-money options and decreases as the option moves deeper into the money or out of the money.

Example: Suppose a call option on Bank Nifty has a gamma of 0.03. If the INR strengthens by 1 point against the USD, the call option's delta will increase by 0.03.

Theta: Theta measures the rate of time decay of an option concerning the passage of one day, assuming all other factors remain constant. It indicates how much an option's value is likely to decrease as time passes.

Theta is particularly significant for options with shorter time to expiration.

Example: Consider a put option on Nifty with a theta of -10. If one day passes, all other factors remaining the same, the put option's value will decrease by 10 INR.

Vega: Vega measures the change in an option's price concerning a 1% change in implied volatility. Implied volatility reflects the market's expectations for future price fluctuations.

Vega is higher for options with longer expiration periods and is more pronounced for at-the-money options.

Example: Suppose a put option on Bank Nifty has a vega of 15. If the implied volatility increases by 1 percentage point, the put option's price will increase by 15 INR.

Rho: Rho represents the change in an option's price concerning a 1% change in the risk-free interest rate.

Rho is more relevant for options with longer maturities, as interest rate changes have a greater impact on options with more time to expiration.

Example: Consider a call option on Nifty with a rho of 8. If the risk-free interest rate increases by 1%, the call option's price will increase by 8 INR.

In summary, understanding Option Greeks is crucial for options traders, as these measures provide insights into how an option's value may change in response to various factors, including changes in the Indian Rupee's value, time decay, implied volatility, and interest rates. Being aware of these factors allows traders to make informed decisions when trading Nifty or Bank Nifty options in the context of the Indian Rupee market.

## 1.2 Option Trading Mechanics in Indian Markets

Option trading mechanics in Indian markets follow specific rules and procedures set by the Securities and Exchange Board of India (SEBI) and stock exchanges like the National Stock Exchange (NSE) and Bombay Stock Exchange (BSE). Let's explore the key aspects of option trading mechanics in the Indian markets:

Types of Options Traded: Indian markets primarily trade European-style options. European options can only be exercised on the expiration date, while American-style options can be exercised any time before or on the expiration date.

Option Contracts: Each option contract in India typically represents the right to buy or sell 100 units of the underlying asset. So, when you trade one option contract, you are effectively dealing with 100 shares or a multiple of the underlying asset, depending on the asset type.

Expiration Cycle: Options in Indian markets have three expiration cycles - the near-month (current month), the next-month, and the far-month (third-month) contracts. Options expire on the last Thursday of each month. If the last Thursday is a trading holiday, the expiration date is the previous trading day.

Strike Prices: Indian markets generally offer multiple strike prices for both call and put options. The strike prices are pre-determined and available at set intervals from the current market price of the underlying asset.

Trading Hours: Options trading in Indian markets takes place during regular trading hours, which is generally from 9:15 AM to 3:30 PM (Indian Standard Time) on trading days. There are pre-opening and post-closing sessions as well.

Option Premiums: Option buyers pay a premium to option sellers. The premium is the cost of holding the option and is influenced by factors like the underlying asset's price, time to expiration, implied volatility, and interest rates.

Order Types: Traders can place various types of option orders, including market orders (buy or sell at the current market price), limit orders (buy or sell at a specified price or better), and stop-loss orders (triggered when the asset price reaches a specified level).

Settlement Method: In Indian markets, options are cash-settled, which means that upon exercise or expiration, the settlement is done in cash rather than physical delivery of the underlying asset. The settlement amount is calculated based on the difference between the option's strike price and the closing price of the underlying asset on the expiration day.

Exercise and Assignment: Option holders can exercise their right to buy or sell the underlying asset on or before the expiration date. However, most options in India are settled without physical delivery, as traders tend to square off their positions before the expiration.

Margin Requirements: Option trading requires initial margins, which vary depending on the underlying asset and the level of volatility. The margins serve as collateral to cover potential losses.

Market Regulation: SEBI and stock exchanges regulate option trading to ensure fair practices and investor protection. There are position limits on option contracts to prevent market manipulation.

Option trading in Indian markets offers significant opportunities for hedging, speculation, and risk management. However, it involves risks, and traders need to have a good understanding of option mechanics, risk management strategies, and market dynamics before engaging in option trading activities. It's advisable to consult with a qualified financial advisor or broker for personalized guidance.

1.3 Importance of Options Trading Strategies:

Options trading strategies play a crucial role in the success of traders and investors in the financial markets. While options offer various opportunities for hedging, speculation, and risk management, employing appropriate strategies enhances the chances of achieving financial objectives. Here are some key reasons highlighting the importance of options trading strategies:

Risk Management: Options strategies allow traders to manage risk effectively. Strategies like buying protective puts or using collar strategies can help protect a portfolio from significant losses during market downturns.

Profit Potential: Options provide traders with the potential for higher returns compared to traditional investments. Leveraged strategies like buying call options or employing vertical spreads offer the opportunity for substantial profits with a limited initial investment.

Hedging and Insurance: Options can act as insurance policies for a portfolio, providing protection against adverse price movements in the underlying assets. Traders can hedge their positions using options to offset potential losses.

Flexibility: Options strategies offer versatility, allowing traders to adapt to various market scenarios. Traders can create strategies suitable for bullish, bearish, or neutral market outlooks.

Income Generation: Options strategies like covered calls enable investors to generate additional income by selling call options against existing stock positions. This can be particularly beneficial in sideways or slightly bullish markets.

Volatility Management: Options strategies can help traders take advantage of changes in market volatility. Strategies like straddles and strangles profit from significant price swings, while volatility-selling strategies aim to profit from relatively stable market conditions.

Diversification: Integrating options trading strategies into a diversified investment portfolio can add another layer of diversification, potentially reducing overall portfolio risk.

Customization: Traders can tailor options strategies to suit their risk tolerance, financial goals, and market outlook. The ability to customize strategies allows for a personalized approach to trading.

Speculation: Options provide an efficient way to speculate on short-term price movements without the need to own the underlying asset. Traders can benefit from market fluctuations with limited capital exposure.

Risk-Reward Management: Options trading strategies enable traders to manage their risk-reward ratios effectively. By selecting strategies with favorable risk-reward profiles, traders can optimize their potential returns while limiting potential losses.

## 1.4 Risks and Rewards of Options Trading:

Like any financial instrument, options trading involves inherent risks and rewards. Understanding these aspects is essential for traders to make informed decisions and manage their investments prudently. Here's a closer look at the risks and rewards of options trading:

Risks:

Limited Time: Options have expiration dates, and if the underlying asset doesn't move favorably before expiration, the option may expire worthless, resulting in a loss of the premium paid.

Price Movements: Options are sensitive to price movements of the underlying asset. If the price moves against the option holder's favor, the option's value may decrease rapidly.

Implied Volatility: Changes in implied volatility can impact option prices. A decrease in volatility can lead to a decline in option premiums, affecting profitability.

Margin Requirements: Trading options on margin involves the risk of higher losses if the position moves unfavorably. Inadequate margin maintenance may lead to margin calls.

Assignment Risk: Option sellers face the risk of being assigned to fulfill their contractual obligations if the option is exercised by the buyer.

Complex Strategies: Some options trading strategies can be complex, and traders must fully understand the mechanics and potential outcomes before implementing them.

Rewards:

Leveraged Returns: Options offer the potential for higher returns compared to traditional investments, as traders can control larger positions with a smaller upfront investment.

Diversification: Options can enhance portfolio diversification and risk management by adding non-correlated assets to a portfolio.

Flexibility: Traders have the flexibility to create and customize strategies based on their market outlook and risk tolerance.

Income Generation: Certain options strategies, such as covered calls, provide opportunities for additional income generation.

Speculative Opportunities: Options allow traders to speculate on short-term price movements without owning the underlying asset, providing potential profit opportunities in various market conditions.

Risk Management: Options strategies can help manage risk effectively and protect portfolios from significant losses.

Conclusion: Options trading offers unique opportunities and challenges to investors and traders. By employing well-thought-out options trading strategies, market participants can enhance their potential for profit, manage risk, and achieve their financial goals. However, it is essential to understand the risks involved and to approach options trading with proper education, discipline, and risk management techniques. Consulting with financial professionals and conducting thorough research is crucial for success in the options market.

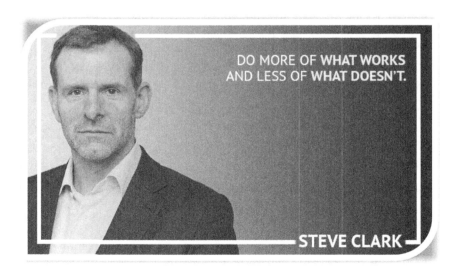

DO MORE OF **WHAT WORKS** AND LESS OF **WHAT DOESN'T.**

STEVE CLARK

## Chapter 2: Getting Started with Options Trading

### 2.1 Setting/Opening up a Trading Account:

Before engaging in options trading in the Indian share market, Nifty, Bank Nifty, or currency options, the first step is to open a trading account with a registered stockbroker or financial institution. Here's a detailed guide on setting up a trading account:

Choose a Reputable Broker: Research and select a reputable broker that offers options trading facilities. Ensure the broker is SEBI registered and provides user-friendly trading platforms.

Gather Required Documents: Prepare necessary documents, such as proof of identity (PAN card, Aadhar card, passport, etc.), proof of address (utility bills, bank statements, etc.), and a passport-sized photograph.

Online or Offline Account Opening: Many brokers offer online account opening. Fill out the application form, attach the required documents, and submit them online. Alternatively, you can visit the broker's office to open an account offline.

Verification Process: The broker will verify the provided documents and may conduct a Know Your Customer (KYC) process to comply with regulatory requirements.

Fund Your Account: Once the account is approved, fund it with the desired amount. Some brokers may offer a virtual/demo account for practice before using real funds.

### 2.2 Option Symbols and Expiration Dates:

In the Indian share market, Nifty, Bank Nifty, and currency options are identified using unique symbols. Understanding option symbols and expiration dates is crucial for placing accurate trades. Option symbols for Nifty and Bank Nifty options follow a standardized format that includes various parameters to represent the specific option contract. Here's how the option symbols are typically structured for Nifty and Bank Nifty options:

Nifty Options:

The option symbol for Nifty options consists of several components:

Underlying Asset Identifier: The symbol "NIFTY" represents the underlying index, Nifty 50.

Expiration Date Code: The expiration date code represents the month and year of expiration. It consists of three letters, where the first two letters represent the month and the third letter represents the year. For example, "JAN" represents January and "23" represents the year 2023.

Option Type Indicator: The option type indicator specifies whether the option is a call or put. The letter "CE" is used for call options, while "PE" is used for put options.

Strike Price: The strike price is represented numerically. It indicates the price at which the option can be exercised. For example, if the strike price is 15,000, it would be represented as "15000".

Putting all the components together, a complete option symbol for a Nifty call option expiring in January 2023 with a strike price of 15,000 would look like this: NIFTY23JAN15000CE.

Bank Nifty Options:

Similar to Nifty options, Bank Nifty options also follow a standardized symbol format:

Underlying Asset Identifier: The symbol "BANKNIFTY" represents the underlying index, Bank Nifty.

Expiration Date Code: The expiration date code follows the same structure as Nifty options, representing the month and year of expiration.

Option Type Indicator: The option type indicator uses "CE" for call options and "PE" for put options.

Strike Price: The strike price is represented numerically.

A complete option symbol for a Bank Nifty put option expiring in January 2023 with a strike price of 35,000 would look like this: BANKNIFTY23JAN35000PE.

It's important to note that option symbols may vary slightly based on different exchanges and brokers. Always refer to the specific guidelines and conventions provided by your trading platform or broker when identifying and trading options.

## 2.3 Option Chains and Quotes

Option chains and quotes provide traders with essential information about available options contracts and their prices. Consider the following details about option chains and quotes:

Option Chains: Option chains are tables that display all available options contracts for a particular underlying asset. They typically include information such as strike prices, expiration dates, bid and ask prices, volume, open interest, and implied volatility.

Strike Prices: Option chains list strike prices, which represent the price at which the underlying asset can be bought (call options) or sold (put options) if the option is exercised.

Bid and Ask Prices: The bid price is the highest price a buyer is willing to pay for the option, while the ask price is the lowest price a seller is willing to accept. The difference between the bid and ask prices is known as the bid-ask spread.

Volume and Open Interest: Volume refers to the number of contracts traded during a particular time period, while open interest represents the total number of outstanding contracts. Higher volume and open interest indicate greater liquidity.

Implied Volatility: Option chains often provide implied volatility, which represents the market's expectation of future price volatility. Implied volatility can impact option prices and can be used to assess the relative attractiveness of different options contracts.

Real-Time Quotes: Option chains may display real-time or delayed quotes. Real-time quotes provide the most up-to-date information but may come with additional costs or account requirements.

Option chains and quotes serve as valuable tools for analyzing available options contracts, identifying potential trading opportunities, and assessing market sentiment.

## 2.4 Placing Option Trades:

After understanding option symbols, expiration dates, option chains, and quotes, traders can place option trades. Here's how to place option trades in the Indian share market:

Log in to the trading account and access the trading platform.

Search for the desired underlying asset (e.g., Nifty, Bank Nifty, or currency pair) and choose the option contract with the preferred strike price and expiration date.

Select the appropriate option strategy (e.g., buying call/put, selling covered calls, and employing spreads) based on the market outlook and risk tolerance.

Enter the number of option contracts to buy or sell and review the order.

Choose the order type (market order or limit order) and click "Submit" to place the trade.

Placing option trades involves executing buy or sell orders for specific options contracts. Consider the following details about placing option trades:

Order Types: Options trades can be executed using various order types, including market orders, limit orders, stop orders, and more. Market orders are executed at the current market price, while limit orders allow traders to specify the maximum price they are willing to pay or the minimum price they are willing to accept.

Option Trading Levels: Brokers may assign different trading levels to options accounts based on the trader's experience and financial situation. Higher trading levels allow for more complex options strategies. Traders should be aware of their approved trading level before placing trades.

Order Entry: Enter the option symbol, specify the number of contracts, and choose the appropriate order type when placing a trade. Double-check all details to ensure accuracy before submitting the order.

Order Execution: Once the order is submitted, the brokerage firm's system will attempt to execute the trade based on the specified order instructions. Options trades are typically executed on options exchanges, where buyers and sellers are matched.

Confirmation and Settlement: After the trade is executed, a trade confirmation is provided, detailing the transaction details. Settlement of options trades occurs within a specific time frame, usually one business day after the trade.

It is crucial to understand the mechanics of placing option trades and be familiar with the order types offered by the brokerage firm. Traders should always review and confirm trade details before submitting orders.

## 2.5 Understanding Trading Platforms and Tools:

Trading platforms and tools play a significant role in options trading. Indian brokers provide advanced trading platforms that offer a range of features and tools to facilitate informed decision-making. Options trading platforms provide the necessary tools and features for traders to analyze, monitor, and execute options trades. Here's what to understand about trading platforms:

Real-time Data: Trading platforms provide real-time market data, including option prices, bid-ask spreads, volume, and open interest. Traders can use this data to analyze market conditions and execute trades.

Option Calculators: Option calculators help calculate option premiums, Greeks (Delta, Gamma, Theta, Vega, and Rho), and potential profit or loss for different option strategies.

Virtual Trading: Some platforms offer virtual trading or demo accounts for practice without risking real money. This allows traders to gain experience before trading with real funds.

Platform Features: Options trading platforms offer a range of features, including real-time market data, option chains, charting tools, order entry interfaces, research resources, and risk management tools. These features help traders analyze options contracts, monitor positions, and execute trades.

Options Analysis Tools: Options trading platforms often provide advanced options analysis tools, such as options calculators, probability calculators, options chains, and implied volatility tools. These tools assist traders in evaluating potential risks and rewards, as well as identifying suitable options strategies.

Charting and Technical Analysis: Many options trading platforms include charting tools and technical analysis indicators. These features help traders analyze historical price data, identify trends, and make informed trading decisions.

Order Management: Options trading platforms allow traders to manage their open positions, monitor their portfolio, and adjust orders as needed. They provide access to order history, position details, and profit/loss calculations.

Mobile Trading: Some brokerage firms offer mobile trading apps, allowing traders to access their options trading accounts and execute trades on the go. Mobile trading apps provide flexibility and convenience for active traders.

Education and Resources: Options trading platforms often provide educational resources, including tutorials, webinars, and articles, to help traders learn about options trading strategies, risk management, and market analysis techniques.

Paper Trading: Some platforms offer paper trading or virtual trading accounts, allowing traders to practice trading options without risking real money. Paper trading is an excellent way for beginners to gain experience and test strategies before trading with real funds.

Choosing the right options trading platform is crucial for traders to effectively analyze, execute, and manage their options trades. Traders should consider factors such as platform usability, available features, research tools, and customer support when selecting a platform.

2.6 Commonly Used Option Trading Terms:

Understanding commonly used option trading terms is essential for effective communication and decision-making. Here are some key terms used in option trading in the Indian share market:

Strike Price: The pre-determined price at which the underlying asset can be bought or sold.

Premium: The price paid or received to buy or sell an option contract.

In-the-Money (ITM): An option that has intrinsic value. For call options, ITM refers to the underlying asset's price being above the strike price. For put options, ITM means the underlying asset's price is below the strike price.

At-the-Money (ATM): An option with a strike price that is equal to the current market price of the underlying asset.

Out-of-the-Money (OTM): An option with no intrinsic value. For call options, OTM means the underlying asset's price is below the strike price. For put options, OTM means the underlying asset's price is above the strike price.

Implied Volatility (IV): The market's expectation of future price fluctuations of the underlying asset, as implied by option prices.

Delta: The change in option price concerning a $1 change in the underlying asset's price.

Gamma: The rate of change of an option's delta concerning a $1 change in the underlying asset's price.

Theta: The rate of time decay of an option as each day passes.

Vega: The change in option price concerning a 1% change in implied volatility.

Rho: The change in option price concerning a 1% change in the risk-free interest rate.

Conclusion: Getting started with options trading in the Indian share market, Nifty, Bank Nifty, and currency options involves setting up a trading account, understanding option symbols and expiration dates, analyzing option chains and quotes, and placing option trades using trading platforms and tools. It is essential to familiarize oneself with commonly used option trading terms to communicate effectively and make informed decisions. With a solid understanding of these fundamentals, traders can embark on their options trading journey with confidence and competence.

## Chapter 3: Option Strategies for Beginners

### 3.1 Buying Call Options

Buying call options is a straightforward bullish strategy that allows traders to profit from an expected increase in the price of the underlying asset. When buying a call option, the trader pays a premium to the option seller (writer) for the right to buy the underlying asset at the strike price before or on the expiration date.

Example: Tata Motors Call Option

Suppose the current market price of Tata Motors shares is Rs. 500. A trader buys one Tata Motors call option with a strike price of Rs. 520 and an expiration date one month from now. If, at expiration, the market price of Tata Motors shares is Rs. 550, the call option is "in the money." The trader can exercise the option, buying Tata Motors shares at the lower strike price of Rs. 520 and selling them in the market at Rs. 550, making a profit of Rs. 30 per share (Rs. 550 - Rs. 520).

Scenario 1 (Profit): If Tata Motors' share price continues to rise and is above the strike price of Rs. 520 at expiration, the trader can exercise the option and profit from the price difference.

Scenario 2 (Loss): If Tata Motors' share price remains below the strike price of Rs. 520 at expiration, the call option would expire worthless, and the trader would lose the premium paid for the option.

### 3.2 Buying Put Options

Buying put options is a bearish strategy used when a trader expects the price of the underlying asset to decrease. When buying a put option, the trader pays a premium to the option seller for the right to sell the underlying asset at the strike price before or on the expiration date.

Example: Infosys Put Option

Suppose the current market price of Infosys shares is Rs. 1,500. A trader buys one Infosys put option with a strike price of Rs. 1,400 and an expiration date one month from now. If, at expiration, the market price of Infosys shares is Rs. 1,300, the put option is "in the money." The trader can exercise the option, selling Infosys shares at the higher strike price of Rs. 1,400 instead of the lower market price, avoiding a loss of Rs. 100 per share (Rs. 1,400 - Rs. 1,300).

Scenario 1 (Profit): If Infosys' share price continues to fall and is below the strike price of Rs. 1,400 at expiration, the trader can exercise the option and profit from the price difference.

Scenario 2 (Loss): If Infosys' share price remains above the strike price of Rs. 1,400 at expiration, the put option would expire worthless, and the trader would lose the premium paid for the option.

### 3.3 Covered Call Strategy

The covered call strategy involves holding a long position in the underlying asset and simultaneously selling call options against it. This strategy is used when the trader has a neutral to slightly bullish outlook on the underlying asset.

Example: HDFC Covered Call

Suppose a trader owns 100 shares of HDFC Ltd., which are currently trading at Rs. 2,000 per share. The trader decides to sell one HDFC call option with a strike price of Rs. 2,200 and an expiration date one month from now. The premium received for selling the call option is Rs. 50.

Scenario 1 (Profit): If HDFC's share price remains below the strike price of Rs. 2,200 at expiration, the call option would expire worthless. The trader keeps the premium of Rs. 50 per share, which adds to their income from holding the HDFC shares.

Scenario 2 (Loss): If HDFC's share price rises above the strike price of Rs. 2,200 at expiration, the call option would be "in the money," and the buyer may exercise the option. In this case, the trader would be obligated to sell the HDFC shares at Rs. 2,200, which is lower than the market price. However, the premium received from selling the call option would help offset some of the losses.

### 3.4 Protective Put Strategy

The protective put strategy involves buying put options to protect an existing long position in the underlying asset. This strategy is used when the trader is concerned about potential downside risk in their portfolio.

Example: Reliance Protective Put

Suppose a trader owns 100 shares of Reliance Industries (RIL), which are currently trading at Rs. 2,000 per share. The trader decides to buy one RIL put option with a strike price of Rs. 1,900 and an expiration date one month from now. The premium paid for buying the put option is Rs. 30.

Scenario 1 (Profit): If RIL's share price remains above the strike price of Rs. 1,900 at expiration, the put option would expire worthless. The trader's loss from the premium paid would be limited, and they would continue to hold the RIL shares.

Scenario 2 (Loss): If RIL's share price falls below the strike price of Rs. 1,900 at expiration, the put option would be "in the money," and the trader can exercise the option. The trader can sell the RIL shares at Rs. 1,900, which is higher than the market price, limiting their losses.

3.5 The Bull Call Spread

The bull call spread is a moderately bullish strategy that involves buying a call option with a lower strike price and simultaneously selling a call option with a higher strike price. This strategy is used when the trader expects a moderate increase in the price of the underlying asset.

Example: Maruti Suzuki Bull Call Spread

Suppose the current market price of Maruti Suzuki shares is Rs. 7,000. A trader executes the following options transactions:

Buys one Maruti Suzuki call option with a strike price of Rs. 6,800 and an expiration date one month from now. The premium paid for buying this call option is Rs. 150.

Sells one Maruti Suzuki call option with a strike price of Rs. 7,200 and an expiration date one month from now. The premium received for selling this call option is Rs. 100.

Scenario 1 (Profit): If, at expiration, the market price of Maruti Suzuki shares is above the higher strike price of Rs. 7,200, both call options would be "in the money." The trader can exercise the lower strike call option and buy the Maruti Suzuki shares at Rs. 6,800, then immediately sell it at the market price, which would be higher. The profit from the difference in strike prices (Rs. 400) would be reduced by the net premium paid (Rs. 50), resulting in a net profit of Rs. 350.

Scenario 2 (Loss): If the market price of Maruti Suzuki shares remains below the lower strike price of Rs. 6,800 at expiration, both call options would expire worthless, and the trader would lose the net premium paid of Rs. 50.

## 3.6 The Bear Put Spread

The bear put spread is a moderately bearish strategy that involves buying a put option with a higher strike price and simultaneously selling a put option with a lower strike price. This strategy is used when the trader expects a moderate decline in the price of the underlying asset.

Example: HCL Technologies Bear Put Spread

Suppose the current market price of HCL Technologies shares is Rs. 1,500. A trader executes the following options transactions:

Buys one HCL Technologies put option with a strike price of Rs. 1,600 and an expiration date one month from now. The premium paid for buying this put option is Rs. 100.

Sells one HCL Technologies put option with a strike price of Rs. 1,400 and an expiration date one month from now. The premium received for selling this put option is Rs. 50.

Scenario 1 (Profit): If, at expiration, the market price of HCL Technologies shares is below the lower strike price of Rs. 1,400, both put options would be "in the money." The trader can exercise the higher strike put option and sell the HCL Technologies shares at Rs. 1,600, which is higher than the market price. The profit from the difference in strike prices (Rs. 200) would be reduced by the net premium paid (Rs. 50), resulting in a net profit of Rs. 150.

Scenario 2 (Loss): If the market price of HCL Technologies shares remains above the higher strike price of Rs. 1,600 at expiration, both put options would expire worthless, and the trader would lose the net premium paid of Rs. 50.

## 3.7 Bullish and Bearish Vertical Spreads

Vertical spreads involve buying and selling call or put options of the same type (both calls or both puts) but with different strike prices. These spreads are classified into two types based on the outlook of the trader:

a) Bullish Vertical Spreads: Bullish vertical spreads involve buying a lower strike option and simultaneously selling a higher strike option. This strategy is used when the trader is moderately bullish on the underlying asset.

Example: Mahindra & Mahindra (M&M) Bullish Vertical Spread

Suppose the current market price of M&M shares is Rs. 800. A trader executes the following options transactions:

Buys one M&M call option with a strike price of Rs. 780 and an expiration date one month from now. The premium paid for buying this call option is Rs. 30.

Sells one M&M call option with a strike price of Rs. 820 and an expiration date one month from now. The premium received for selling this call option is Rs. 15.

Scenario 1 (Profit): If, at expiration, the market price of M&M shares is above the higher strike price of Rs. 820, both call options would be "in the money." The trader can exercise the lower strike call option and buy the M&M shares at Rs. 780, then immediately sell it at the market price, which would be higher. The profit from the difference in strike prices (Rs. 40) would be reduced by the net premium paid (Rs. 15), resulting in a net profit of Rs. 25.

Scenario 2 (Loss): If the market price of M&M shares remains below the lower strike price of Rs. 780 at expiration, both call options would expire worthless, and the trader would lose the net premium paid of Rs. 15.

b) Bearish Vertical Spreads: Bearish vertical spreads involve buying a higher strike option and simultaneously selling a lower strike option. This strategy is used when the trader is moderately bearish on the underlying asset.

Example: Sun Pharmaceutical (Sun Pharma) Bearish Vertical Spread

Suppose the current market price of Sun Pharma shares is Rs. 500. A trader executes the following options transactions:

Buys one Sun Pharma put option with a strike price of Rs. 520 and an expiration date one month from now. The premium paid for buying this put option is Rs. 25.

Sells one Sun Pharma put option with a strike price of Rs. 480 and an expiration date one month from now. The premium received for selling this put option is Rs. 15.

Scenario 1 (Profit): If, at expiration, the market price of Sun Pharma shares is below the lower strike price of Rs. 480, both put options would be "in the money." The trader can exercise the higher strike put option and sell the Sun Pharma shares at Rs. 520, which is higher than the market price. The profit from the difference in strike prices (Rs. 40) would be reduced by the net premium paid (Rs. 10), resulting in a net profit of Rs. 30.

Scenario 2 (Loss): If the market price of Sun Pharma shares remains above the higher strike price of Rs. 520 at expiration, both put options would expire worthless, and the trader would lose the net premium paid of Rs. 10.

### 3.8 Collars and Risk Management

A collar is a risk management strategy that involves combining the purchase of protective put options with the sale of covered call options. This strategy is used when the trader wants to protect an existing long position in the underlying asset while limiting potential upside gains.

Example: Wipro Collar

Suppose a trader owns 100 shares of Wipro, which are currently trading at Rs. 300 per share. The trader executes the following options transactions:

Buys one Wipro put option with a strike price of Rs. 280 and an expiration date one month from now. The premium paid for buying this put option is Rs. 5.

Sells one Wipro call option with a strike price of Rs. 320 and an expiration date one month from now. The premium received for selling this call option is Rs. 3.

By implementing the collar strategy, the trader has limited their potential downside risk with the protective put and generated some income from the covered call. The net cost of the collar is Rs. 2 (Rs. 5 - Rs. 3) per share.

Scenario 1 (Profit): If Wipro's share price falls below the strike price of Rs. 280 at expiration, the put option would be "in the money." The trader can exercise the put option and sell the Wipro shares at Rs. 280, avoiding a larger loss than if they hadn't used the collar strategy.

Scenario 2 (Loss): If Wipro's share price rises above the strike price of Rs. 320 at expiration, the call option would be "in the money," and the buyer may exercise the option. In this case, the trader would be obligated to sell the Wipro shares at Rs. 320, which is lower than the market price.

However, the premium received from selling the call option would help offset some of the losses.

The collar strategy is an effective way to protect an existing position from significant downside risk while still participating in potential upside gains within a limited range.

Conclusion: These option strategies provide beginners with a range of techniques to approach the dynamic Indian share market, Nifty, and Bank Nifty. Each strategy comes with its unique risk and reward profile, and traders should carefully assess their market outlook, risk tolerance, and financial goals before choosing a strategy. Additionally, it's crucial to implement proper risk management and continuously educate oneself about the options market to make informed decisions and navigate the complexities of options trading successfully.

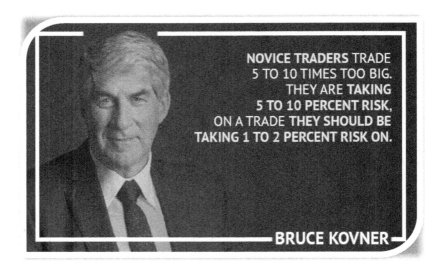

NOVICE TRADERS TRADE 5 TO 10 TIMES TOO BIG. THEY ARE TAKING 5 TO 10 PERCENT RISK, ON A TRADE THEY SHOULD BE TAKING 1 TO 2 PERCENT RISK ON.

— BRUCE KOVNER —

## Chapter 4: Advanced Option Trading Strategies

4.1 Long Straddle Strategy

The long straddle strategy involves buying both a call option and a put option with the same strike price and expiration date. This strategy is used when the trader expects significant price volatility in the underlying asset but is uncertain about the direction of the price movement.

Example: Long Straddle on Infosys

Suppose the current market price of Infosys shares is Rs. 1,500. A trader executes the following options transactions:

Buys one Infosys call option with a strike price of Rs. 1,500 and an expiration date one month from now. The premium paid for buying this call option is Rs. 50.

Buys one Infosys put option with a strike price of Rs. 1,500 and an expiration date one month from now. The premium paid for buying this put option is Rs. 40.

Scenario 1 (Profit): If, at expiration, the market price of Infosys shares is significantly higher or lower than Rs. 1,500, one of the options will be "in the money," and the other will expire worthless. The profit potential is unlimited in either direction, as long as the move is substantial enough to cover the combined cost of both options.

Scenario 2 (Loss): If the market price of Infosys shares remains close to Rs. 1,500 at expiration, both options would expire worthless, and the trader would lose the net premium paid for both options.

4.2 Long Strangle Strategy

The long strangle strategy is similar to the long straddle, but instead of using the same strike price for both options, the trader buys a call option with a higher strike price and a put option with a lower strike price. This strategy is also used when the trader anticipates significant price volatility but is uncertain about the direction of the price movement.

Example: Long Strangle on Nifty

Suppose the current market price of Nifty index is 15,000. A trader executes the following options transactions:

Buys one Nifty call option with a strike price of 15,200 and an expiration date one month from now. The premium paid for buying this call option is Rs. 100.

Buys one Nifty put option with a strike price of 14,800 and an expiration date one month from now. The premium paid for buying this put option is Rs. 90.

Scenario 1 (Profit): If, at expiration, the Nifty index is significantly higher than 15,200 or lower than 14,800, one of the options will be "in the money," and the other will expire worthless. The profit potential is unlimited in either direction, as long as the move is substantial enough to cover the combined cost of both options.

Scenario 2 (Loss): If the Nifty index remains within a narrow range around 15,000 at expiration, both options would expire worthless, and the trader would lose the net premium paid for both options.

4.3 Iron Condors and Iron Butterflies

Iron condors and iron butterflies are advanced strategies that involve combining multiple options with different strike prices to create a net credit position. These strategies are used when the trader expects the underlying asset's price to remain within a specific range and wants to generate income from the premiums received.

a) Iron Condor:

An iron condor involves selling a call spread (bear call spread) and a put spread (bull put spread) with the same expiration date but different strike prices.

Example: Iron Condor on Bank Nifty

Suppose the current market price of Bank Nifty is 35,000. A trader executes the following options transactions:

Sells one Bank Nifty call option with a strike price of 35,500 and buys one Bank Nifty call option with a strike price of 36,000. The premium received for selling the call option is Rs. 150, and the premium paid for buying the call option is Rs. 50.

Sells one Bank Nifty put option with a strike price of 34,500 and buys one Bank Nifty put option with a strike price of 34,000. The premium received for selling the put option is Rs. 120, and the premium paid for buying the put option is Rs. 70.

The net premium received from the call spread (Rs. 100) and the put spread (Rs. 50) results in a total credit of Rs. 150.

Scenario 1 (Profit): If the Bank Nifty index remains between the strike prices of 34,500 and 35,500 at expiration, all options in the iron condor would expire worthless, and the trader would keep the net premium received of Rs. 150 as profit.

Scenario 2 (Loss): If the Bank Nifty index moves significantly beyond either the upper or lower strike price at expiration, one of the options in the iron condor would be "in the money," and the trader would face potential losses.

b) Iron Butterfly:

An iron butterfly is similar to an iron condor but involves selling a call spread and a put spread with the same middle strike price.

Example: Iron Butterfly on Nifty

Suppose the current market price of Nifty index is 15,000. A trader executes the following options transactions:

Sells one Nifty call option with a strike price of 15,100 and buys one Nifty call option with a strike price of 15,200. The premium received for selling the call option is Rs. 120, and the premium paid for buying the call option is Rs. 80.

Sells one Nifty put option with a strike price of 14,900 and buys one Nifty put option with a strike price of 14,800. The premium received for selling the put option is Rs. 100, and the premium paid for buying the put option is Rs. 70.

The net premium received from the call spread (Rs. 40) and the put spread (Rs. 30) results in a total credit of Rs. 70.

Scenario 1 (Profit): If the Nifty index remains close to the middle strike price of 15,000 at expiration, all options in the iron butterfly would expire worthless, and the trader would keep the net premium received of Rs. 70 as profit.

Scenario 2 (Loss): If the Nifty index moves significantly beyond either the upper or lower strike price at expiration, one of the options in the iron butterfly would be "in the money," and the trader would face potential losses.

## 4.4 Calendar Spread Strategy

The calendar spread strategy involves buying and selling options with the same strike price but different expiration dates. This strategy is used when the trader expects minimal price movement in the underlying asset in the short term but anticipates larger moves in the longer term.

Example: Calendar Spread on Reliance Industries (RIL)

Suppose the current market price of RIL shares is Rs. 2,000. A trader executes the following options transactions:

Buys one RIL call option with a strike price of Rs. 2,000 and an expiration date three months from now. The premium paid for buying this call option is Rs. 200.

Sells one RIL call option with a strike price of Rs. 2,000 and an expiration date one month from now. The premium received for selling this call option is Rs. 100.

The net premium paid for the calendar spread is Rs. 100.

Scenario 1 (Profit): If the market price of RIL shares remains close to Rs. 2,000 at the near-month expiration, the near-month call option would expire worthless, and the trader could potentially sell another call option with a later expiration to collect additional premiums. The trader's profit potential lies in collecting multiple premiums while holding the longer-term call option.

Scenario 2 (Loss): If the market price of RIL shares moves significantly beyond Rs. 2,000 at the near-month expiration, the near-month call option would be "in the money," and the trader could face potential losses on the longer-term call option.

## 4.5 Diagonal Spreads

Diagonal spreads are similar to calendar spreads but involve different strike prices in addition to different expiration dates. This strategy provides more flexibility and potential for profit if the underlying asset's price moves moderately in either direction.

Example: Diagonal Spread on Nifty

Suppose the current market price of Nifty index is 15,000. A trader executes the following options transactions:

Buys one Nifty call option with a strike price of 14,800 and an expiration date three months from now. The premium paid for buying this call option is Rs. 120.

Sells one Nifty call option with a strike price of 15,200 and an expiration date one month from now. The premium received for selling this call option is Rs. 80.

The net premium paid for the diagonal spread is Rs. 40.

Scenario 1 (Profit): If the Nifty index remains close to 15,000 at the near-month expiration, the near-month call option would expire worthless, and the trader could potentially sell another call option with a later expiration and different strike price to collect additional premiums. The trader's profit potential lies in collecting multiple premiums while holding the longer-term call option.

Scenario 2 (Profit): If the Nifty index moves moderately above or below 15,000 at the near-month expiration, one of the options would be "in the money," and the trader could realize a profit based on the price difference and premium collected.

Scenario 3 (Loss): If the Nifty index moves significantly beyond either the upper or lower strike price at the near-month expiration, the trader could face potential losses on the longer-term call option.

4.6 Ratio Spreads

Ratio spreads involve an uneven number of options to create a strategy that is either bullish or bearish, depending on the trader's outlook. This strategy is used when the trader expects significant price movement in the underlying asset but is uncertain about the direction.

a) Bull Ratio Spread:

A bull ratio spread involves buying more call options than the number of put options sold. This strategy benefits from bullish price movement while limiting potential losses.

Example: Bull Ratio Spread on Tata Motors

Suppose the current market price of Tata Motors shares is Rs. 300. A trader executes the following options transactions:

Buys two Tata Motors call options with a strike price of Rs. 290 and an expiration date one month from now. The premium paid for buying each call option is Rs. 10.

Sells one Tata Motors call option with a strike price of Rs. 300 and an expiration date one month from now. The premium received for selling this call option is Rs. 15.

The net premium paid for the bull ratio spread is Rs. 5 (Rs. 10 + Rs. 10 - Rs. 15).

Scenario 1 (Profit): If Tata Motors' share price rises above Rs. 300 at expiration, the trader can exercise the two lower strike call options and buy Tata Motors shares at Rs. 290 each. The trader can then sell the shares in the market at the higher market price, making a profit from the price difference.

Scenario 2 (Loss): If Tata Motors' share price remains below Rs. 300 at expiration, both the lower strike call options and the sold call option would expire worthless, and the trader would lose the net premium paid of Rs. 5.

b) Bear Ratio Spread:

A bear ratio spread involves buying more put options than the number of call options sold. This strategy benefits from bearish price movement while limiting potential losses.

Example: Bear Ratio Spread on Infosys

Suppose the current market price of Infosys shares is Rs. 1,500. A trader executes the following options transactions:

Buys two Infosys put options with a strike price of Rs. 1,550 and an expiration date one month from now. The premium paid for buying each put option is Rs. 20.

Sells one Infosys put option with a strike price of Rs. 1,500 and an expiration date one month from now. The premium received for selling this put option is Rs. 30.

The net premium received for the bear ratio spread is Rs. 10 (Rs. 20 + Rs. 20 - Rs. 30).

Scenario 1 (Profit): If Infosys' share price falls below Rs. 1,500 at expiration, the trader can exercise the two higher strike put options and sell Infosys shares at Rs. 1,550 each. The trader can then buy the shares back in the market at the lower market price, making a profit from the price difference.

Scenario 2 (Loss): If Infosys' share price remains above Rs. 1,500 at expiration, both the higher strike put options and the sold put option would expire worthless, and the trader would lose the net premium received of Rs. 10.

4.7 Synthetic Positions

Synthetic positions are options strategies that replicate the risk and reward profile of another options strategy or the underlying asset. These strategies are used when the trader wants to mimic the exposure of a particular position without directly buying or selling the underlying asset or options.

Example: Synthetic Long Stock

A synthetic long stock position involves buying a call option and simultaneously selling a put option with the same strike price and expiration date. This strategy replicates the risk and reward profile of owning the underlying asset.

Suppose the current market price of HDFC Ltd. shares is Rs. 2,000. A trader executes the following options transactions:

Buys one HDFC call option with a strike price of Rs. 2,000 and an expiration date one month from now. The premium paid for buying this call option is Rs. 50.

Sells one HDFC put option with a strike price of Rs. 2,000 and an expiration date one month from now. The premium received for selling this put option is Rs. 40.

The net premium paid for the synthetic long stock is Rs. 10 (Rs. 50 - Rs. 40).

Scenario 1 (Profit): If HDFC's share price rises above Rs. 2,000 at expiration, the call option would be "in the money," and the trader can exercise the option and buy HDFC shares at Rs. 2,000 each. The trader's profit potential is unlimited, as they own the shares at a fixed price.

Scenario 2 (Loss): If HDFC's share price falls below Rs. 2,000 at expiration, the put option would be "in the money," and the buyer may exercise the option. The trader would be obligated to buy the HDFC shares at Rs. 2,000, which is higher than the market price. However, the premium received from selling the put option would help offset some of the losses.

## 4.8 Strategies for Market Volatility

### 4.8.1 Dealing with High Volatility in the Market

High market volatility can lead to significant price swings and uncertainty, making option trading riskier. Here are some ways to manage high volatility:

a) Reduce Position Size: In times of high volatility, consider reducing the size of your option positions to limit potential losses.

b) Trade Liquid Options: Focus on options with good liquidity to ensure you can enter and exit positions efficiently.

c) Use Options Spreads: Employ options spreads to reduce the cost of trades and control risk. Spreads involve buying and selling multiple options simultaneously.

### 4.8.2 Volatility-Based Options Trading Strategies

Incorporating volatility-based strategies can help traders take advantage of the changing market conditions:

a) Straddle: The long straddle strategy (buying both a call and a put option) benefits from increased volatility, as it allows traders to profit from significant price swings regardless of the direction.

b) Strangle: The long strangle strategy (buying both a call and a put option with different strike prices) also benefits from increased volatility, as it leverages larger price movements.

c) Iron Condor: The iron condor strategy can be adjusted for high volatility. Traders can widen the spread between the call and put options to capture more significant price fluctuations.

### 4.8.3 Hedging Techniques during Market Turmoil

During periods of market turmoil, options can be used as hedging instruments to protect against potential losses in a portfolio:

a) Protective Put: Buying put options on individual stocks or indices can act as insurance, providing a hedge against a decline in the market.

b) Collars: Implementing collars on positions can limit downside risk while still allowing for some upside potential.

c) Volatility Index (VIX) Options: VIX options are linked to the market's volatility index and can serve as a direct hedge against market volatility.

## 4.9 Options Trading for Income Generation

### 4.9.1 Income-Generating Strategies with Options

Options can be utilized to generate income in addition to capital appreciation. Income-generating strategies involve selling options to collect premiums:

a) Covered Calls: Selling covered call options against existing long positions generates income from the premiums received. This strategy works well in a neutral to slightly bullish market environment.

b) Cash-Secured Puts: Selling cash-secured put options allows traders to generate income while potentially acquiring the underlying asset at a discount if the options are exercised.

### 4.9.2 Covered Calls and Cash-Secured Puts for Income

Example: Income-Generating Strategy on TCS

Suppose a trader owns 100 shares of Tata Consultancy Services (TCS), which are currently trading at Rs. 3,000 per share. The trader executes the following options transactions:

a) Covered Call: Sells one TCS call option with a strike price of Rs. 3,200 and an expiration date one month from now. The premium received for selling the call option is Rs. 100.

b) Cash-Secured Put: Sells one TCS put option with a strike price of Rs. 2,800 and an expiration date one month from now. The premium received for selling the put option is Rs. 80.

Scenario 1 (Profit): If the market price of TCS shares remains below Rs. 3,200 at expiration, the call option would expire worthless, and the trader would keep the premium received from selling the call option (Rs. 100).

Scenario 2 (Profit): If the market price of TCS shares remains above Rs. 2,800 at expiration, the put option would expire worthless, and the trader would keep the premium received from selling the put option (Rs. 80).

Scenario 3 (Loss): If the market price of TCS shares falls below Rs. 2,800 at expiration, the put option would be "in the money," and the trader may be obligated to buy 100 shares of TCS at Rs. 2,800 each. However, the premium received from selling the put option (Rs. 80) would help offset some of the losses.

### 4.9.3 Dividend Arbitrage with Options

Dividend arbitrage involves capitalizing on the difference between the dividend payments on the underlying asset and the premiums received from selling options.

Example: Dividend Arbitrage on Hindustan Unilever (HUL)

Suppose HUL announces a dividend of Rs. 10 per share, payable in one month. The current market price of HUL shares is Rs. 2,000. A trader executes the following options transactions:

a) Sells one HUL call option with a strike price of Rs. 2,050 and an expiration date one month from now. The premium received for selling the call option is Rs. 40.

The dividend arbitrage strategy aims to capitalize on the dividend payment while collecting premiums from selling call options.

Scenario 1 (Profit): If the market price of HUL shares remains below Rs. 2,050 at expiration, the call option would expire worthless, and the trader would keep the premium received from selling the call option (Rs. 40). Additionally, the trader would receive the dividend payment of Rs. 10 per share.

Scenario 2 (Loss): If the market price of HUL shares rises above Rs. 2,050 at expiration, the call option would be "in the money," and the trader may face potential losses. However, the dividend payment of Rs. 10 per share would help offset some of the losses.

Conclusion: Advanced option trading strategies offer traders a variety of tools to navigate the complexities of the Indian share market, Nifty, and Bank Nifty while taking advantage of different market conditions. These strategies come with their unique risk and reward profiles, and traders should carefully consider their market outlook, risk tolerance, and financial goals before implementing them. Additionally, continuous learning and risk management are essential components of successful option trading.

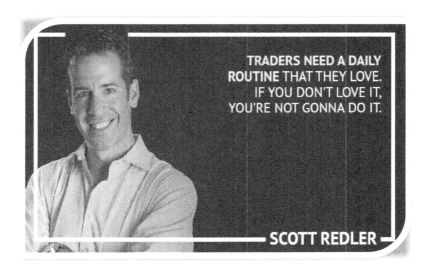

TRADERS NEED A DAILY ROUTINE THAT THEY LOVE. IF YOU DON'T LOVE IT, YOU'RE NOT GONNA DO IT.

— SCOTT REDLER —

# Chapter 5: Options Trading with Indian Shares

## 5.1 Analyzing Indian Stocks for Options Trading

Analyzing Indian stocks before engaging in options trading is essential for making informed and profitable trading decisions. Here are the key factors to consider when analyzing Indian stocks for options trading:

a) Liquidity: Liquidity is one of the most critical factors to consider when trading options. Look for stocks with active options contracts and sufficient trading volume. High liquidity ensures that you can enter and exit positions easily without significant price slippage.

b) Implied and Historical Volatility: Volatility is a measure of the stock's price fluctuations. Implied volatility represents the market's expectation of future price volatility, while historical volatility reflects past price movements. Higher volatility often translates to higher options premiums and potential trading opportunities.

c) Fundamental Analysis: Evaluate the company's financial health, earnings growth, profitability, debt levels, and competitive positioning. Strong fundamentals suggest a stable underlying stock and can provide more predictable price movements.

d) Technical Analysis: Use technical indicators, chart patterns, and trend analysis to identify entry and exit points for options trades. Technical analysis helps traders understand the stock's price trends and potential reversals.

e) Sector Performance: Consider the performance of the sector to which the stock belongs. Strong sector performance can provide tailwinds for individual stocks, while weak sector performance can act as a headwind.

f) Market Sentiment: Pay attention to market sentiment, macroeconomic factors, and global market trends. Positive market sentiment can drive stocks higher, while negative sentiment can lead to price declines.

g) Dividend Dates: Be aware of dividend announcement dates and ex-dividend dates. Dividends can impact options pricing, especially for American-style options.

h) Event Risks: Take note of upcoming events, such as earnings announcements, mergers and acquisitions, regulatory decisions, and geopolitical events, that may significantly impact the stock's price.

i) Options Chain Analysis: Review the options chain for the stock to understand the available strike prices, expiration dates, and premiums for call and put options. Look for strike prices that align with your trading strategy and risk tolerance.

j) Open Interest and Volume: Analyze the open interest and daily trading volume for options contracts. High open interest indicates active participation in those contracts, while increasing or decreasing volume can indicate changing market sentiment.

k) Market Maker and Bid-Ask Spread: Consider the market maker's role and the bid-ask spread. A narrow bid-ask spread indicates a liquid market, while wider spreads can lead to higher trading costs.

l) Options Greeks: Familiarize yourself with options Greeks, such as delta, gamma, theta, vega, and rho. These measures provide insights into the sensitivity of options prices to changes in underlying stock price, time, volatility, and interest rates.

Case Study: Analyzing XYZ Ltd. for Options Trading

XYZ Ltd. is a leading Indian company in the IT sector. The stock is currently trading at Rs. 1,500 per share. Let's analyze XYZ Ltd. based on the factors mentioned above:

Liquidity: Check the trading volume and open interest for XYZ Ltd.'s options. Ensure that there is sufficient liquidity and active participation in options trading.

Volatility: Analyze the implied volatility of XYZ Ltd.'s options to gauge the market's expectation of future price movements. Look at the historical volatility to understand past price fluctuations.

Fundamental Analysis: Review XYZ Ltd.'s financial statements, earnings reports, and industry rankings. Assess the company's growth prospects and competitive advantages.

Technical Analysis: Examine XYZ Ltd.'s price charts and technical indicators to identify trends and potential support and resistance levels.

Sector Performance: Consider the performance of the IT sector as it can influence XYZ Ltd.'s stock price.

Market Sentiment: Analyze general market sentiment and macroeconomic factors that may impact XYZ Ltd.'s stock price.

Dividend Dates: Check if there are any upcoming dividend announcements that could affect options pricing.

Event Risks: Be aware of any scheduled events, such as earnings releases or regulatory decisions, that may cause price volatility.

Options Chain Analysis: Review the options chain for XYZ Ltd. to identify suitable strike prices and expiration dates for your trading strategy.

Open Interest and Volume: Look at the open interest and volume of options contracts to gauge market participation.

Market Maker and Bid-Ask Spread: Consider the role of market makers and evaluate the bid-ask spread for XYZ Ltd.'s options.

Options Greeks: Calculate the options Greeks to understand the sensitivity of the options' prices to changes in underlying stock price, time, and volatility.

By conducting a comprehensive analysis of XYZ Ltd., you can make informed decisions about trading options on this stock. Remember that no single factor should drive your decision-making; instead, consider all relevant factors together to develop a well-rounded trading strategy.

Analyzing Indian stocks for options trading involves a multi-dimensional approach that considers liquidity, volatility, fundamentals, technicals, market sentiment, and various other factors. This detailed analysis empowers traders to identify potential trading opportunities and manage risks effectively. Implementing a systematic analysis process and staying updated with market developments are crucial for success in options trading with Indian shares. As you gain experience, refine your analysis techniques to adapt to changing market conditions and improve your options trading performance.

5.2 Best Practices for Option Trading with Indian Shares

To enhance your success in options trading with Indian shares, consider the following best practices:

a) Risk Management: Set a maximum risk level for each trade and avoid overcommitting to any single trade. Use stop-loss orders to limit potential losses. Implement robust risk management practices to protect your capital. Avoid risking more than a predetermined percentage of your trading capital on any single trade. Set stop-loss orders to limit potential losses in adverse market conditions.

b) Diversification: Avoid concentrating your trades in a single stock or sector. Diversification helps spread risk across different assets and reduces the impact of a single stock's price movement. Avoid overexposure to a single stock or sector. Diversify your options trading positions across different shares and industries to spread risk effectively.

c) Education: Continuously educate yourself about options trading strategies, market dynamics, and risk management techniques. Stay updated on changes in market regulations and practices. Before venturing into options trading, invest time in learning about options, how they work, and various trading strategies. Understand options pricing, Greeks, and the factors that influence options premiums. Continuously educate yourself on new developments in the options market.

d) Start Small: If you are new to options trading, start with a small capital allocation and gradually increase it as you gain experience and confidence.

e) Paper Trading: Practice options trading strategies in a simulated environment before risking real money. Paper trading allows you to test your strategies without incurring losses.

f) Keep Emotions in Check: Emotions can cloud judgment and lead to impulsive decisions. Stick to your trading plan and avoid making emotional trades.

g) Start with a Clear Strategy: Define your trading objectives and risk tolerance. Develop a clear trading strategy that aligns with your goals. Decide whether you want to trade options for speculation, hedging, or income generation, and select appropriate strategies accordingly.

h) Use Liquid Stocks and Options: Focus on trading options of liquid and actively traded Indian shares. Liquid options have tight bid-ask spreads, which allow for better execution and reduce trading costs.

i) Use Stop-Loss Orders: Place stop-loss orders on your options positions to automatically exit a trade if the market moves against you. This helps limit losses and prevents emotional decision-making.

j) Manage Position Size: Avoid allocating an excessive portion of your trading capital to any single options trade. Consider position sizing based on the risk-reward profile of the trade.

k) Avoid Emotional Trading: Emotions can cloud judgment and lead to impulsive decisions. Stick to your trading plan and avoid making emotionally driven trades.

l) Regularly Monitor Positions: Stay actively involved in monitoring your options positions. Be prepared to adjust or close trades based on changing market conditions or your original trading plan.

m) Paper Trade: If you are new to options trading, consider paper trading first. Paper trading allows you to practice trading strategies in a risk-free simulated environment before risking real money.

n) Review and Learn from Trades: Analyze your past trades to identify strengths and weaknesses in your trading strategy. Learn from both successful and unsuccessful trades to refine your approach.

o) Be Wary of Illiquid Options: Avoid trading options with low liquidity, as they may have wider bid-ask spreads and limited trading opportunities.

p) Understand Expiration and Assignment: Be aware of the expiration dates of your options contracts. Decide in advance whether you want to exercise options or let them expire. If you are short options, be prepared for potential assignment if they are in-the-money at expiration.

q) Consider Options Expiry Timing: Select options contracts with expiration dates that align with your trading timeframe and market outlook. Short-term traders may prefer weekly or monthly options, while long-term investors may choose options with several months to expiration.

r) Stay Updated: Stay informed about company earnings, economic data releases, and other market-moving events that may impact Indian shares and options prices.

s) Avoid Chasing Losses: Avoid the temptation to chase losses by increasing position sizes or taking higher risks. Stick to your trading plan and avoid letting emotions dictate your trading decisions.

Option trading with Indian shares can be a rewarding endeavor if approached with discipline, a well-thought-out strategy, and adherence to best practices. Educate yourself about options, practice risk management, diversify your positions, and continuously monitor your trades. By implementing these best practices and staying updated with market developments, you can improve your chances of success in options trading with Indian shares. Remember that options trading involves risks, and it's essential to exercise caution and prudence in your trading approach.

## 5.3 Case Studies with Indian Share Options

Case Study 1: Reliance Industries (RIL) Call Option

Suppose the current market price of RIL shares is Rs. 2,000, and you expect the stock to rise in the short term due to positive news about a new product launch. You decide to buy one RIL call option with a strike price of Rs. 2,100 and an expiration date one month from now. The premium paid for buying this call option is Rs. 80.

Scenario 1 (Profit): If RIL's share price rises above Rs. 2,180 (Rs. 2,100 + Rs. 80) at expiration, the call option would be "in the money." You can exercise the option and buy RIL shares at Rs. 2,100 each, then sell them in the market at the higher market price, making a profit from the price difference.

Scenario 2 (Loss): If RIL's share price remains below Rs. 2,100 at expiration, the call option would expire worthless, and you would lose the premium paid of Rs. 80.

Case Study 2: Tata Motors (TML) Put Option

Suppose the current market price of TML shares is Rs. 300, and you expect the stock to decline in the short term due to disappointing quarterly earnings. You decide to buy one TML put option with a strike price of Rs. 280 and an expiration date one month from now. The premium paid for buying this put option is Rs. 10.

Scenario 1 (Profit): If TML's share price falls below Rs. 270 (Rs. 280 - Rs. 10) at expiration, the put option would be "in the money." You can exercise the option and sell TML shares at Rs. 280 each, then buy them back in the market at the lower market price, making a profit from the price difference.

Scenario 2 (Loss): If TML's share price remains above Rs. 280 at expiration, the put option would expire worthless, and you would lose the premium paid of Rs. 10.

Options trading with Indian shares can be a lucrative way to participate in the Indian stock market while managing risk. By analyzing Indian stocks, adhering to best practices, and learning from case studies, traders can make informed decisions and build a successful options trading strategy.

However, it's essential to remember that options trading carry inherent risks, and traders should exercise caution and prudence in their approach. Continuous education, discipline, and risk management are key to achieving long-term success in options trading with Indian shares.

FRANKLY, I DON'T SEE MARKETS, I SEE RISKS, REWARDS, AND MONEY.

LARRY HITE

## Chapter 6: Options Trading with Nifty

### 6.1 Nifty Options: An Overview

Nifty options are options contracts based on the National Stock Exchange's (NSE) Nifty 50 Index, which represents the performance of the 50 largest and most liquid stocks in the Indian equity market. Nifty options offer traders the opportunity to speculate on the direction of the Nifty index or hedge their equity portfolios against market movements. Here's an overview of Nifty options:

Types of Nifty Options: Nifty options come in two types - call options and put options. Call options give the holder the right, but not the obligation, to buy the Nifty index at a predetermined price (strike price) on or before the expiration date. Put options give the holder the right, but not the obligation, to sell the Nifty index at a predetermined price (strike price) on or before the expiration date.

Contract Size: Each Nifty options contract represents a specified lot size of the Nifty index. The lot size may vary from time to time, depending on the exchange's regulations.

Expiration: Nifty options have monthly expirations. The last Thursday of every month is the expiration day for Nifty options. If the last Thursday is a trading holiday, the previous trading day is considered the expiration day.

European-Style Options: Nifty options are European-style options, which means they can only be exercised on the expiration day, not before.

Strike Prices: Nifty options have multiple strike prices available, with some being closer to the current Nifty index level and others being further away. Traders can select strike prices based on their trading strategy and market outlook.

Premium: The premium is the price paid by the option buyer to the option seller to acquire the option contract. It represents the cost of the option and is influenced by factors such as the Nifty index level, time to expiration, implied volatility, and interest rates.

### 6.2 Trading Nifty Call and Put Options

Trading Nifty call and put options involves speculating on the Nifty index's future direction or using options to hedge existing positions. Here's an overview of trading Nifty call and put options:

Nifty Call Options: Traders buy Nifty call options if they anticipate the Nifty index will rise. By buying call options, traders have the potential to profit from Nifty's upward price movement while limiting their maximum loss to the premium paid for the options.

Nifty Put Options: Traders buy Nifty put options if they expect the Nifty index will decline. By buying put options, traders have the potential to profit from Nifty's downward price movement while limiting their maximum loss to the premium paid for the options.

Writing (Selling) Nifty Options: Traders can also write (sell) Nifty options to earn premiums. Writing Nifty call options is a bullish strategy, while writing Nifty put options is a bearish strategy. However, writing options carries unlimited risk, and traders must maintain sufficient margins to cover potential losses.

6.3 Hedging with Nifty Options

Nifty options can be used for hedging purposes to protect an equity portfolio from adverse market movements. Here are common hedging strategies using Nifty options:

Protective Put: Investors with an equity portfolio can buy Nifty put options to protect against potential losses if the Nifty index declines. If the Nifty falls, the put option's value increases, offsetting some of the losses in the portfolio.

Covered Call: Investors holding Nifty index positions can write (sell) Nifty call options against their Nifty holdings. The premium received from selling the call options provides some downside protection if the Nifty index falls.

Collar: A collar strategy involves buying a Nifty put option to protect against downside risk while simultaneously writing (selling) a Nifty call option to generate income. This strategy provides a limited profit potential and downside protection within a specific range of Nifty index levels.

6.4 Case Studies with Nifty Options

Case Study 1: Nifty Call Option for Speculation

Suppose the Nifty index is currently trading at 15,000, and you expect the Nifty to rise in the coming weeks due to positive economic data. You decide to buy one Nifty call option with a strike price of 15,200 and an expiration date one month from now. The premium paid for buying this call option is Rs. 150.

Scenario 1 (Profit): If the Nifty index rises above 15,350 (15,200 + 150) at expiration, the call option would be "in the money." You can exercise the option and buy the Nifty index at 15,200, then sell it in the market at the higher market price, making a profit from the price difference.

Scenario 2 (Loss): If the Nifty index remains below 15,200 at expiration, the call option would expire worthless, and you would lose the premium paid of Rs. 150.

Case Study 2: Protective Put for Hedging

Suppose you have an equity portfolio worth Rs. 5,00,000, and you are concerned about a potential market downturn. You decide to buy one Nifty put option with a strike price of 14,800 and an expiration date one month from now. The premium paid for buying this put option is Rs. 200.

Scenario 1 (Protection): If the Nifty index falls below 14,800 at expiration, the put option would be "in the money." The put option's value would increase, offsetting some of the losses in your equity portfolio.

Scenario 2 (No Protection Needed): If the Nifty index remains above 14,800 at expiration, the put option would expire worthless. However, your equity portfolio may still benefit from any positive market movements.

Nifty options provide traders with the opportunity to speculate on the direction of the Nifty index or hedge their equity portfolios against market movements. Traders can trade Nifty call and put options based on their market outlook, and investors can use Nifty options for hedging purposes to protect their equity portfolios. Understanding Nifty options' mechanics and employing appropriate strategies can enhance the effectiveness of trading and hedging with Nifty options. As with any options trading, it is essential to manage risks, stay informed about market developments, and continuously educate yourself to make well-informed decisions.

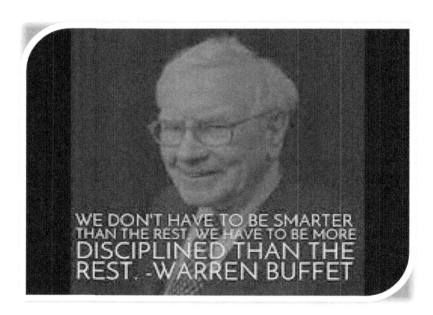

# Chapter 7: Options Trading with Bank Nifty

## 7.1 Bank Nifty Options: An Introduction

Bank Nifty options are options contracts based on the NSE's Bank Nifty Index, which comprises the most liquid and actively traded banking stocks in India. Trading Bank Nifty options allows market participants to speculate on the banking sector's performance or hedge their exposure to banking stocks. Here's an introduction to Bank Nifty options:

Bank Nifty Index: The Bank Nifty Index represents the price movement of select banking stocks listed on the NSE. It provides an overview of the banking sector's performance in the Indian stock market.

Types of Bank Nifty Options: Similar to Nifty options, Bank Nifty options come in two types - call options and put options. Call options give the holder the right, but not the obligation, to buy the Bank Nifty Index at a predetermined price (strike price) on or before the expiration date. Put options give the holder the right, but not the obligation, to sell the Bank Nifty Index at a predetermined price (strike price) on or before the expiration date.

Contract Size: Each Bank Nifty options contract represents a specified lot size of the Bank Nifty Index.

Expiration: Bank Nifty options have monthly expirations. The last Thursday of every month is the expiration day for Bank Nifty options. If the last Thursday is a trading holiday, the previous trading day is considered the expiration day.

European-Style Options: Bank Nifty options are European-style options, which means they can only be exercised on the expiration day, not before.

Strike Prices: Bank Nifty options have multiple strike prices available, with some being closer to the current Bank Nifty Index level and others being further away.

Premium: The premium is the price paid by the option buyer to the option seller to acquire the option contract. It represents the cost of the option and is influenced by factors such as the Bank Nifty Index level, time to expiration, implied volatility, and interest rates.

## 7.2 Strategies for Trading Bank Nifty Options

Trading Bank Nifty options involves employing various strategies based on the trader's market outlook and risk tolerance. Here are some common strategies for trading Bank Nifty options:

Long Call: Traders can buy Bank Nifty call options if they anticipate the Bank Nifty Index will rise. By buying call options, traders have the potential to profit from Bank Nifty's upward price movement while limiting their maximum loss to the premium paid for the options.

Long Put: Traders can buy Bank Nifty put options if they expect the Bank Nifty Index will decline. By buying put options, traders have the potential to profit from Bank Nifty's downward price movement while limiting their maximum loss to the premium paid for the options.

Covered Call: Investors holding Bank Nifty Index positions can write (sell) Bank Nifty call options against their holdings. The premium received from selling the call options provides some downside protection if the Bank Nifty Index falls.

Protective Put: Investors with a Bank Nifty Index position can buy Bank Nifty put options to protect against potential losses if the Bank Nifty Index declines.

Bull Call Spread: This strategy involves buying one Bank Nifty call option with a lower strike price and simultaneously selling another call option with a higher strike price. It is a limited-risk, limited-reward strategy used when a moderate rise in the Bank Nifty Index is expected.

Bear Put Spread: This strategy involves buying one Bank Nifty put option with a higher strike price and simultaneously selling another put option with a lower strike price. It is a limited-risk, limited-reward strategy used when a moderate decline in the Bank Nifty Index is expected.

## 7.3 Leveraging Bank Nifty Options for Income Generation

Bank Nifty options can also be utilized for income generation through various strategies:

Covered Call: Investors holding banking stocks can write (sell) Bank Nifty call options against their holdings to generate income from the premiums received.

Cash-Secured Put: Investors can write (sell) Bank Nifty put options while setting aside cash equal to the strike price as collateral. If the options expire worthless, the premium received becomes income for the investor.

Iron Condor: This is an income-generating strategy that involves selling both a bear call spread and a bull put spread simultaneously on Bank Nifty options.

7.4 Case Studies with Bank Nifty Options

Case Study 1: Bank Nifty Long Call Option

Suppose the Bank Nifty Index is currently trading at 34,000, and you expect it to rise in the near term due to positive economic data. You decide to buy one Bank Nifty call option with a strike price of 34,500 and an expiration date one month from now. The premium paid for buying this call option is Rs. 200.

Scenario 1 (Profit): If the Bank Nifty Index rises above 34,700 (34,500 + 200) at expiration, the call option would be "in the money." You can exercise the option and buy the Bank Nifty Index at 34,500, then sell it in the market at the higher market price, making a profit from the price difference.

Scenario 2 (Loss): If the Bank Nifty Index remains below 34,500 at expiration, the call option would expire worthless, and you would lose the premium paid of Rs. 200.

Case Study 2: Covered Call with Bank Nifty Options

Suppose you own 100 shares of a banking stock with a current market price of Rs. 1,500 per share. You decide to write (sell) one Bank Nifty call option with a strike price of 36,000 and an expiration date one month from now. The premium received for selling this call option is Rs. 300.

Scenario 1 (Profit): If the Bank Nifty Index remains below 36,000 at expiration, the call option would expire worthless, and you would keep the premium received of Rs. 300.

Scenario 2 (Loss): If the Bank Nifty Index rises above 36,000 at expiration, the call option would be "in the money," and the option buyer may exercise the option. You would be obligated to sell the Bank Nifty Index at 36,000, limiting your potential profit from the underlying shares' price appreciation.

Bank Nifty options provide traders and investors with opportunities to speculate on the banking sector's performance or hedge their exposure to banking stocks. Understanding the mechanics of Bank Nifty options and employing appropriate trading and income-generating strategies can enhance the effectiveness of trading with Bank Nifty options. As with any options trading, it is essential to manage risks, stay informed about market developments, and continuously educate yourself to make well-informed decisions.

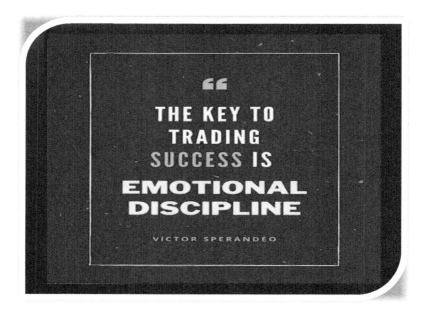

## Chapter 8: Technical Analysis for Option Trading

8.1 Understanding Charts and Trends

Technical analysis is a method of evaluating and predicting future price movements of financial assets, including stocks, indices, and commodities, based on historical price data and patterns. In options trading, technical analysis helps traders identify potential entry and exit points for options positions. Let's dive into the key components of technical analysis:

Charts: Charts are graphical representations of an asset's historical price data over a specific time period. The most common types of charts used in technical analysis are line charts, bar charts, and candlestick charts.

Line Chart: A line chart connects the closing prices of the asset over a specified period, creating a simple line that helps identify trends.

Bar Chart: A bar chart displays the high, low, open, and close prices for each period using vertical bars. The high and low prices are represented by the top and bottom of the bar, while the open and close prices are marked by small horizontal lines on the left and right sides of the bar, respectively.

Candlestick Chart: A candlestick chart is similar to a bar chart but visually more appealing. It uses candlestick-shaped bars to represent the price movement within a specific time frame. Each candlestick shows the open, high, low, and close prices for that period. If the close price is higher than the open price, the candlestick is typically colored green or white, indicating a bullish period. If the close price is lower than the open price, the candlestick is colored red or black, indicating a bearish period.

Trends: Trends represent the general direction in which an asset's price is moving over time. Identifying trends is crucial in options trading as it helps traders determine the overall market sentiment and the most appropriate options strategies to use.

Upward Trend (Bullish): An upward trend occurs when the asset's price forms higher highs and higher lows. Traders may consider buying call options or using bullish options strategies in an upward trend.

Downward Trend (Bearish): A downward trend occurs when the asset's price forms lower highs and lower lows. Traders may consider buying put options or using bearish options strategies in a downward trend.

Sideways Trend (Neutral): A sideways trend occurs when the asset's price moves within a relatively narrow range without forming clear higher highs or lower lows. Traders may consider using range-bound options strategies in a sideways trend.

Technical analysts often use trendlines to visually identify and follow trends. A trend line is a straight line drawn on the chart that connects multiple highs or lows, indicating the direction of the trend.

8.2 Support and Resistance Levels

Support and resistance levels are critical concepts in technical analysis. They are specific price levels on a chart where the asset's price tends to stop, reverse, or consolidate. Traders use support and resistance levels to make informed decisions about entering or exiting options positions.

Support: Support levels are price levels where the asset's price has historically stopped falling and bounced back higher. Traders believe that buying interest outweighs selling pressure at support levels, causing the price to reverse. When an asset's price approaches a strong support level, traders may consider buying call options or implementing bullish options strategies.

Resistance: Resistance levels are price levels where the asset's price has historically stopped rising and pulled back. Traders believe that selling pressure outweighs buying interest at resistance levels, causing the price to reverse. When an asset's price approaches a strong resistance level, traders may consider buying put options or implementing bearish options strategies.

Support and resistance levels can be identified by examining historical price data on the chart. The more times a price level acts as a support or resistance, the stronger it is believed to be.

8.3 Moving Averages and Oscillators

Moving Averages: Moving averages are trend-following indicators that smooth out price data over a specified period. They help traders identify the underlying trend and filter out short-term price fluctuations.

Simple Moving Average (SMA): The SMA is the average of an asset's prices over a specific number of periods. It provides a basic moving average line on the chart.

Exponential Moving Average (EMA): The EMA gives more weight to recent prices, making it more responsive to changes in price trends compared to the SMA.

Traders use moving averages to identify trend reversals or confirm trend direction. When the asset's price crosses above its moving average, it may signal a bullish trend, while a cross below the moving average may signal a bearish trend.

Oscillators: Oscillators are technical indicators that fluctuate within a bounded range, typically between 0 and 100. They help traders identify overbought and oversold conditions in the market, which can indicate potential trend reversals.

Relative Strength Index (RSI): The RSI compares the magnitude of recent price gains to recent price losses to determine if the asset is overbought or oversold. An RSI value above 70 indicates an overbought condition, while an RSI below 30 indicates an oversold condition.

Moving Average Convergence Divergence (MACD): The MACD is a trend-following oscillator that consists of two lines - the MACD line and the signal line. Traders look for bullish or bearish crossovers between these lines to identify potential entry and exit points.

8.4 Chart Patterns and Candlestick Analysis

Chart Patterns: Chart patterns are specific formations that appear on price charts and provide clues about the asset's future price direction. Traders use chart patterns to anticipate potential breakouts or breakdowns in the asset's price.

Head and Shoulders: The head and shoulders pattern consists of three peaks, with the middle peak (head) being higher than the other two (shoulders). It indicates a potential trend reversal from bullish to bearish.

Double Tops and Double Bottoms: Double tops are formed when the asset's price reaches a peak, pulls back, and then forms another peak around the same level. Double bottoms are the opposite, with the asset's price forming two troughs around the same level. These patterns suggest potential trend reversals.

Triangles: Triangles are formed when the asset's price forms higher lows and lower highs, creating converging trendlines. Symmetrical triangles suggest a breakout is imminent, while ascending triangles indicate potential bullish breakouts, and descending triangles suggest potential bearish breakouts.

Flags and Pennants: Flags and pennants are short-term continuation patterns that form after a sharp price movement. They indicate a temporary pause before the prevailing trend resumes.

Candlestick Analysis: Candlestick charts provide valuable insights into market sentiment and potential trend reversals. Traders use candlestick patterns to make trading decisions.

Doji: A doji candlestick occurs when the asset's open and close prices are very close or equal, forming a small-bodied candlestick. It indicates indecision in the market and can signal potential trend reversals.

Hammer and Hanging Man: Hammer and hanging man candlesticks have small bodies with long lower wicks. Hammers appear after a downtrend and signal potential bullish reversals, while hanging men appear after an uptrend and signal potential bearish reversals.

Engulfing Patterns: Bullish engulfing patterns occur when a larger bullish candlestick completely engulfs the preceding bearish candlestick, signaling a potential bullish reversal. Bearish engulfing patterns are the opposite and suggest potential bearish reversals.

8.5 Using Technical Indicators with Options

Technical indicators are valuable tools for options traders, helping them make well-informed decisions and gauge market sentiment. Here's how technical indicators can be used with options:

Confirming Trends: Traders use moving averages to identify the underlying trend and align their options trades with the prevailing trend. For example, buying call options in an uptrend or buying put options in a downtrend can be more effective when confirmed by moving average crossovers.

Overbought and Oversold Conditions: Oscillators like the RSI can help traders identify overbought and oversold conditions in the market. When an asset is overbought, traders may consider buying put options, anticipating a potential reversal. Conversely, when an asset is oversold, traders may consider buying call options, anticipating a potential bounce.

Timing Entry and Exit Points: Chart patterns and candlestick analysis can help traders time their entry and exit points for options trades. For example, a bullish candlestick pattern, such as a hammer, may signal a potential call option entry, while a bearish candlestick pattern, such as a shooting star, may signal a potential put option entry.

Technical analysis is a valuable tool for options traders, providing insights into trends, support and resistance levels, and potential entry and exit points for options positions. By understanding charts, recognizing trends, using technical indicators, and analyzing chart patterns and candlestick formations, options traders can make more informed trading decisions. However, it is essential to remember that technical analysis is not foolproof and options trading involves risks. Traders should always use technical analysis in conjunction with other tools and risk management techniques to achieve success in the options market. Continuously educating oneself and staying updated with market developments are vital to becoming a successful options trader using technical analysis.

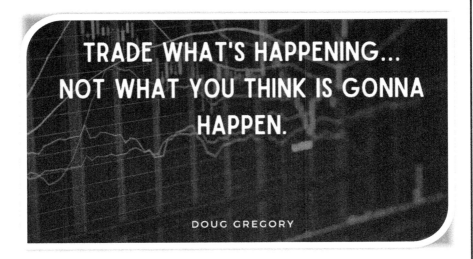

## Chapter 9: Fundamental Analysis for Option Trading

Fundamental analysis is a comprehensive method of evaluating the intrinsic value of financial assets, such as stocks and indices, by analyzing various economic, financial, and industry factors. In the context of the Indian market, fundamental analysis is a crucial tool for options traders seeking to make well-informed decisions about potential price movements and overall market sentiment. Here's an in-depth look at how fundamental analysis applies to option trading in the Indian market:

### 9.1 Economic Indicators and Market News

Economic indicators and market news play a significant role in shaping market sentiment and influencing options prices in the Indian market. As India is a developing economy, economic data and news can have a substantial impact on asset prices. Key economic indicators and market news to consider include:

Gross Domestic Product (GDP) Growth: India's GDP growth rate reflects the overall health of the economy. Positive GDP growth rates signal economic expansion and often lead to a bullish market sentiment, while lower-than-expected GDP growth may lead to a bearish sentiment.

Inflation Rate: The rate of inflation affects the purchasing power of consumers and the cost of living. High inflation rates can impact interest rates and overall economic activity, potentially affecting options pricing.

Interest Rates: The Reserve Bank of India (RBI) sets interest rates, which influence borrowing costs and liquidity in the economy. Changes in interest rates can have a significant impact on market volatility and options prices.

Trade Balance: India's trade balance, which measures the difference between exports and imports, can influence the value of the Indian Rupee and international trade relations. A positive trade balance may lead to a stronger currency and vice versa.

Traders must keep a close eye on economic indicators and market news to gauge the overall macroeconomic environment and potential implications for options positions.

### 9.2 Earnings Reports and Company Analysis

Earnings reports play a crucial role in fundamental analysis, especially for options traders focusing on individual stocks in the Indian market. Strong earnings growth can positively impact a company's stock price, making bullish options strategies more attractive. Conversely, disappointing earnings can lead to bearish options strategies.

Key factors to consider in earnings reports and company analysis include:

Earnings Per Share (EPS): EPS measures a company's profitability by dividing net earnings by the number of outstanding shares. Higher EPS typically leads to increased investor confidence.

Revenue Growth: Steady revenue growth indicates a healthy business, while declining revenue may raise concerns about a company's performance.

Profit Margins: Profit margins reflect a company's efficiency in managing costs. Expanding profit margins are often viewed positively by investors.

Forward Guidance: Companies' future outlook and guidance can significantly impact investor sentiment and options pricing.

Before executing options trades on individual stocks, traders should conduct thorough company analysis and consider the potential impact of earnings reports on their positions.

## 9.3 Event-driven Trading with Options

Event-driven trading involves taking positions based on specific events, such as corporate announcements, economic data releases, policy decisions, or geopolitical developments. These events can lead to significant price movements and increased volatility in the market.

Options can be an efficient tool for capitalizing on event-driven opportunities with limited risk. For example:

Merger or Acquisition: Traders may use options to implement strategies like long straddles or strangles ahead of merger announcements, anticipating substantial price swings.

Regulatory Decisions: Options can help traders hedge against potential losses or speculate on price movements before and after regulatory decisions are made.

Traders must stay alert to upcoming events and their potential impact on the market and specific assets to use options effectively in event-driven trading.

## 9.4 Sector Analysis and ETF Options

Sector analysis involves evaluating specific industries or sectors in the market. Different sectors perform differently under various economic conditions, and understanding sector dynamics can guide options trading strategies.

Exchange-Traded Funds (ETFs) offer an efficient way to gain exposure to entire sectors rather than individual stocks. Options on ETFs allow traders to implement sector-based strategies with reduced risk. For example:

Sector Rotation: Traders can use options on sector-specific ETFs to rotate in and out of sectors based on economic conditions and sector performance.

Hedging Sector Exposure: Options on ETFs can serve as a hedging tool for traders with significant exposure to specific sectors.

Understanding the dynamics of various sectors and using options on sector-specific ETFs can enhance trading opportunities in the Indian market.

## 9.5 Interpreting Options Sentiment

Options sentiment refers to the overall market sentiment derived from options trading activity. It can provide insights into traders' expectations and future market moves. Key aspects of options sentiment in the Indian market include:

Implied Volatility (IV): IV is a measure of the market's expectation for future price fluctuations. High IV indicates expected price volatility, while low IV suggests relatively stable market conditions.

Put-Call Ratio (PCR): PCR is the ratio of open put options to open call options. A high PCR suggests bearish sentiment, while a low PCR indicates bullish sentiment.

Options Volume and Open Interest: High options volume and open interest in specific strike prices can indicate strong support or resistance levels.

Traders should analyze options sentiment alongside other fundamental and technical indicators to make well-informed decisions in the Indian options market.

Fundamental analysis is a vital tool for options traders in the Indian market. By evaluating economic indicators, market news, earnings reports, company performance, and other factors, traders can better understand the underlying value of assets and make more informed options trading decisions. Combining fundamental analysis with technical analysis allows traders to manage risk effectively and seize opportunities in the dynamic and rapidly evolving Indian options market. Continuous education and staying updated with economic and market developments are essential for success in options trading in the Indian market.

## Chapter 10: Risk Management and Position Sizing in the Indian Market

10.1 Setting Risk Tolerance

Setting risk tolerance is a crucial first step in options trading in the Indian market. Traders must determine the level of risk they are comfortable taking on each trade and establish clear guidelines for managing risk. Factors to consider while setting risk tolerance include:

Financial Goals: Define your financial objectives, whether they are short-term gains, long-term growth, or income generation.

Investment Horizon: Consider the time frame for your trades and align your risk tolerance with your trading strategy.

Capital Allocation: Determine the maximum amount of capital you are willing to risk on a single trade or within a specific time frame. This can be a fixed percentage of your total trading capital.

10.2 Diversification and Portfolio Allocation

Diversification is a risk management technique that involves spreading investments across different assets to reduce exposure to any single asset's volatility. In the Indian market, diversification can be achieved by using a mix of options strategies, trading multiple assets or sectors, and varying the expiration dates of options contracts.

Portfolio allocation involves dividing your trading capital among different strategies and assets based on their risk and return characteristics. Diversifying your portfolio helps mitigate the impact of adverse market movements on your overall trading capital.

10.3 Using Stop Losses, Limit Orders, and Trailing Stops

Using stop losses, limit orders, and trailing stops is essential for managing trade execution and limiting potential losses in the Indian market.

Stop Loss: Placing a stop-loss order below the entry price for long positions or above the entry price for short positions triggers a market order to exit the trade if the asset's price reaches the specified stop-loss level. Stop losses help limit losses in case the market moves against the trade.

Limit Order: A limit order is placed to buy or sell options at a specific price or better. It ensures that the trade is executed at the desired price or a more favourable price.

Trailing Stop: A trailing stop follows the asset's price in the direction of the trade. If the price moves favorably, the trailing stop adjusts to a specified percentage or dollar amount below the current price. If the price reverses, the trailing stop remains unchanged. Trailing stops help lock in profits while giving the trade room to move in a favorable direction.

These order types are valuable tools for managing trade execution effectively and protecting against sudden market fluctuations in the Indian market.

## 10.4 Managing Position Sizes

Properly managing position sizes is critical for risk management in options trading. It involves determining the amount of capital allocated to each trade to limit potential losses and maintain consistency in risk exposure. Some position sizing methods for the Indian market include:

Fixed Amount: Allocate a dollar amount for each trade, typically a percentage of your total trading capital.

Fixed Percentage of Capital: Allocate a fixed percentage of your total trading capital for each trade. This approach adjusts position sizes based on changes in capital, preventing overexposure during losing streaks.

Volatility-based Sizing: Adjust position sizes based on the volatility of the underlying asset. Higher volatility assets may require smaller position sizes to manage risk.

By managing position sizes effectively, traders can protect their capital and reduce the impact of potential losses in the Indian market.

## 10.5 Managing Margin and Leverage

Margin and leverage can amplify both gains and losses in options trading. In the Indian market, it is essential to manage margin and leverage prudently to protect capital and avoid excessive risk.

Understand Margin Requirements: Different options strategies have varying margin requirements set by brokers. Be aware of these requirements to avoid unexpected margin calls.

Limit Leverage: Avoid excessive leverage, especially in high-risk strategies like naked options writing, as it can lead to substantial losses.

Consider Risk-to-Reward Ratio: Assess the risk-to-reward ratio of each trade to ensure that the potential gain justifies the leverage used.

Careful management of margin and leverage is crucial for protecting capital and maintaining a sustainable trading approach in the Indian market.

10.6 Hedging and Risk Mitigation

Hedging is a risk management strategy that involves using offsetting positions to protect against potential losses. In the Indian market, hedging can be achieved through various strategies, such as:

Protective Puts: Buying put options to protect a long stock position from a significant downside move.

Covered Calls: Selling call options against a long stock position to generate income and partially offset potential losses.

Collars: Combining long puts and covered calls to limit potential losses while capping potential gains.

Spreads: Implementing vertical spreads (bull call spreads or bear put spreads) to reduce the cost of options positions and manage risk.

Hedging allows traders to protect their portfolios during periods of market uncertainty and volatility in the Indian market.

Risk management and position sizing are paramount for successful options trading in the Indian market. By setting risk tolerance, diversifying the portfolio, using stop losses and limit orders, managing position sizes, and being cautious with margin and leverage, traders can protect their capital and maintain discipline in their approach. Employing hedging strategies can provide additional protection during market turbulence. Remember that options trading involves inherent risks, and no risk management strategy guarantees profits or eliminates all losses. It is essential to combine risk management with sound analysis and a thorough understanding of options strategies to navigate the Indian market successfully. Continuous monitoring and periodic adjustments to risk management practices are crucial for achieving long-term success in options trading in the Indian market.

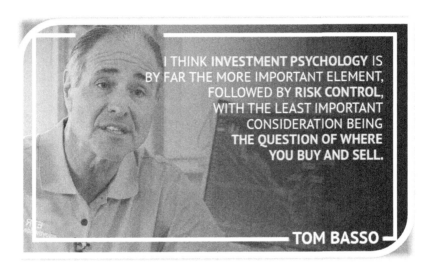

I THINK **INVESTMENT PSYCHOLOGY** IS BY FAR THE MORE IMPORTANT ELEMENT, FOLLOWED BY **RISK CONTROL**, WITH THE LEAST IMPORTANT CONSIDERATION BEING **THE QUESTION OF WHERE** YOU BUY AND SELL.

— **TOM BASSO**

# Chapter 11: Psychology of Option Trading

<u>11.1 Emotions and Decision Making:</u>

The field of behavioural finance has highlighted the significant impact of emotions on financial decision-making, including option trading. Emotions can influence a trader's perception of risk and reward, their ability to stay disciplined, and their willingness to stick to a well-thought-out trading plan. Understanding the role of emotions in decision-making is crucial for traders to make rational and informed choices in the face of market fluctuations. Let's delve deeper into the key emotions that affect option trading decisions:

Fear: Fear is a natural emotional response to perceived threats or uncertainty. In trading, fear often arises from the fear of losses or missing out on potential profits. Fear can lead traders to hesitate or avoid taking advantageous positions, even when their analysis suggests otherwise. This can result in missed opportunities and reduced profitability.

Greed: Greed is the desire for excessive gains or the urge to take on higher risks for potentially higher returns. Traders driven by greed might overleverage their positions or deviate from their trading plan to chase quick profits. This behaviour can expose them to substantial losses if the market moves against them.

Anxiety: Anxiety in trading stems from the uncertainty of the markets and the fear of the unknown. It can lead to a state of constant worry, making it difficult for traders to think clearly and execute their trades effectively. Anxiety may cause traders to close positions prematurely or hold on to losing trades for too long, hoping for a reversal.

Excitement: Excitement arises when traders experience a winning streak or witness significant market movements. While excitement can be motivating, it can also cloud judgment and lead to impulsive decisions. Traders may take on additional risks during periods of excitement, which can backfire when market conditions change.

Regret: Regret is a common emotion experienced after making a losing trade or missing a profitable opportunity. Traders who dwell on past mistakes may become hesitant to take future trades, leading to missed chances for recovery.

Overconfidence: Overconfidence occurs when traders believe they have superior skills or insights, leading them to underestimate market risks.

Overconfident traders may neglect risk management practices and overtrade, increasing their exposure to potential losses.

Managing Emotions in Option Trading:

Develop Self-Awareness: Recognizing and acknowledging emotions as they arise is the first step in managing them effectively. Traders should be mindful of how emotions can influence their decision-making and take a step back to assess their thought process before executing a trade.

Stick to a Trading Plan: Having a well-defined trading plan with clear entry and exit rules can help counteract impulsive decisions driven by emotions. Traders should follow their plan rigorously and avoid deviating from it based on short-term emotions.

Risk Management: Implementing proper risk management techniques, such as setting stop-loss orders, can help traders limit potential losses and alleviate fear. By knowing their acceptable risk levels, traders can approach trading with more confidence.

Keep a Trading Journal: Maintaining a trading journal can help traders track their emotions and analyze how they impact their trading decisions. This self-reflection can provide valuable insights into patterns of behavior and aid in making necessary adjustments to their approach.

Take Breaks and Practice Mindfulness: Engaging in mindfulness exercises and taking breaks during trading sessions can help reduce anxiety and keep traders focused on the present moment. Meditation, deep breathing, or even physical activities can be effective in managing stress.

Learn from Mistakes: Instead of dwelling on losses, view them as opportunities for growth and learning. Analyzing past trades can help identify patterns and mistakes, leading to improvements in future decision-making.

By acknowledging the influence of emotions in option trading and employing strategies to manage them, traders can enhance their decision-making process and increase their chances of success in the market. Emotions will always be a part of trading, but developing emotional intelligence can significantly improve a trader's ability to navigate the challenges of the financial markets effectively.

## 11.2 Maintaining Discipline and Patience:

Maintaining discipline and patience is essential for achieving long-term success in option trading. The financial markets can be highly volatile, and impulsive decisions driven by emotions or the desire for quick profits can lead to significant losses. Here's a detailed look at how traders can cultivate discipline and patience in their trading approach:

Establish a Clear Trading Plan: A well-defined trading plan serves as the foundation for discipline in trading. The plan should outline the trader's objectives, preferred trading strategies, risk tolerance, and specific rules for entering and exiting trades. It should also include a risk management strategy to control the amount of capital risked per trade.

Follow a Rule-Based Approach: Discipline in trading involves adhering to a rule-based approach, where all trading decisions are based on pre-established criteria rather than impulsive reactions to market movements. Traders should set clear entry and exit criteria, and only execute trades that meet these criteria, regardless of emotional impulses.

Avoid Emotional Trading: Emotional trading, driven by fear or greed, can lead to impulsive and irrational decisions. Traders must recognize their emotional triggers and take steps to minimize their impact on trading. Implementing techniques like mindfulness, self-awareness, and regular breaks during trading sessions can help reduce emotional interference.

Use Stop-Loss Orders: Stop-loss orders are an essential risk management tool that helps traders limit potential losses on a trade. Placing stop-loss orders at predetermined levels allows traders to exit a position if the market moves against them, thus preventing significant losses. Adhering to stop-loss levels requires discipline, as it means accepting and acting on losses when necessary.

Set Realistic Expectations: Patience is required to set realistic expectations in option trading. Markets can be unpredictable, and traders should avoid expecting overnight success or huge profits from every trade. Instead, they should focus on consistent and incremental gains over time.

Wait for the Right Opportunities: Patience is especially crucial when waiting for suitable trading opportunities. Traders must resist the temptation to force trades or enter positions without proper analysis. Waiting for high-probability setups based on their trading plan increases the likelihood of successful trades.

Avoid Overtrading: Overtrading is a common pitfall for traders, particularly when they experience a series of small wins. The desire to capitalize on every market move can lead to excessive trading activity, increased transaction costs, and higher exposure to potential losses. Traders should stick to their trading plan and avoid overtrading.

Review and Analyze Trades: Regularly reviewing and analyzing past trades can provide valuable insights into a trader's performance. By objectively evaluating their trading decisions, traders can identify areas for improvement and adjust their strategies accordingly.

Stay Committed to Long-Term Goals: Option trading is a journey that requires commitment to long-term goals. Traders should be patient and persistent, understanding that success may not come immediately. Staying focused on their objectives and trading plan can help traders avoid making impulsive decisions driven by short-term emotions.

Learn from Mistakes: Discipline involves learning from mistakes and not repeating them. Instead of dwelling on losses or missed opportunities, traders should use them as learning experiences to refine their strategies and become better traders over time.

By cultivating discipline and patience in their trading approach, traders can maintain a rational and systematic decision-making process, reduce emotional interference, and improve their overall performance in option trading. Remember that trading is a journey of continuous learning, and embracing discipline and patience can lead to more consistent and sustainable results in the long run.

## 11.3 Handling Losses and Drawdowns:

Handling losses and drawdowns is a critical aspect of successful option trading. Losses are an inherent part of trading, and every trader will experience them at some point. Drawdowns refer to the decline in the value of a trader's account from its peak, and they can occur during losing streaks or unfavourable market conditions. How traders respond to losses and drawdowns can significantly impact their emotional well-being and overall trading performance. Here are some strategies for effectively handling losses and drawdowns in option trading:

Accepting and Embracing Losses: The first step in handling losses is accepting that they are a natural part of trading. No trading strategy is immune to losses, and even the most successful traders experience them. Embracing losses as learning opportunities can help shift the focus from the negative emotions associated with them to identifying areas for improvement.

Implementing Risk Management: Effective risk management is crucial in managing losses and drawdowns. Traders should limit the size of each trade to a percentage of their total capital that they are comfortable risking. Setting stop-loss orders at appropriate levels helps prevent losses from exceeding predetermined risk limits.

Avoiding Revenge Trading: After experiencing a loss, traders may be tempted to engage in revenge trading – attempting to recover the lost capital quickly by taking on additional risk. This behavior often leads to more losses, as it is driven by emotions rather than a well-thought-out trading plan.

Sticking to the Trading Plan: Traders should adhere to their trading plan even after a series of losses. Deviating from the plan in response to losses can lead to impulsive decisions and further losses. Consistently following the trading plan, which includes predefined entry and exit points, helps maintain discipline during drawdowns.

Analyzing Losses: After a losing trade or drawdown period, it is essential to conduct a thorough analysis of the trades to identify potential reasons for the losses. Examining the trade setup, market conditions, and any deviations from the trading plan can provide insights for improvement.

Taking Breaks: During drawdowns or periods of consecutive losses, it's crucial for traders to take breaks to clear their minds and reduce emotional stress. Stepping away from the market for a while can help traders regain focus and approach trading with a fresh perspective.

Managing Position Sizing: To minimize the impact of drawdowns, traders can adjust their position sizes during unfavorable market conditions. Reducing position sizes during challenging periods can help preserve capital and avoid significant drawdowns.

Seeking Support: Sharing experiences with fellow traders or seeking guidance from trading mentors can provide emotional support during tough times. Talking to others who have experienced drawdowns can offer valuable insights and reassurance.

Maintaining Confidence: Experiencing losses or drawdowns can dent a trader's confidence. It's essential to remember that trading performance is a long-term endeavor. Maintaining confidence in one's abilities and the effectiveness of the trading strategy can help navigate through challenging periods.

Focusing on Long-Term Goals: Traders should keep their focus on long-term goals rather than getting bogged down by short-term losses. A series of losses does not necessarily mean a flawed strategy; it could simply be a normal market variation. Trusting in the trading plan and staying committed to long-term goals can help traders remain resilient during drawdowns.

In conclusion, handling losses and drawdowns requires a combination of emotional resilience, risk management, and adherence to a well-defined trading plan. By accepting losses as part of the trading process, implementing effective risk management, and maintaining discipline during challenging times, traders can navigate through drawdowns and continue on their path to success in option trading.

11.4 Developing a Trading Plan

Define Your Objectives: Start by setting clear and realistic trading objectives. Determine what you aim to achieve through option trading – whether it's capital growth, generating income, or hedging existing positions. Your objectives will guide the rest of your trading plan.

Example: The objective is to achieve consistent capital growth by trading Nifty and Bank Nifty options. The trader aims to generate a 20% return on their trading capital in Indian rupees annually.

Assess Your Risk Tolerance: Understand your risk tolerance level – the amount of capital you are willing to risk on each trade and overall in your trading account. This assessment will influence your position sizing and risk management strategies.

Example: The trader has a moderate risk tolerance and is willing to risk up to 2% of their total trading capital in Indian rupees on each Nifty or Bank Nifty options trade.

Choose Your Trading Style and Strategies: Decide on your preferred trading style, such as day trading, swing trading, or position trading. Based on your objectives and risk tolerance, select the option trading strategies that align with your goals. Strategies may include buying calls or puts, spreads, straddles, or combinations of different option contracts.

Example: The trader prefers a combination of day trading and swing trading. For Nifty options, they will use a long straddle strategy during highly volatile events like corporate earnings announcements or major economic releases. For Bank Nifty options, they will focus on short strangles during periods of low volatility.

Establish Entry and Exit Criteria: Define specific entry and exit points for your trades. For example, you may decide to enter a trade when a certain technical indicator confirms a trend, or exit a trade when the option reaches a predetermined profit target or stop-loss level.

Example for Nifty: The trader will enter a long straddle position on Nifty options when there is a significant event with potential for market-moving volatility, such as quarterly earnings releases for Nifty 50 companies. They will exit the straddle position if the Nifty index shows a significant directional move or if the options' premiums reach a predetermined profit target.

Example for Bank Nifty: The trader will enter a short strangle position on Bank Nifty options when the implied volatility is low, and the index is trading within a well-defined range. They will exit the short strangle position if the Bank Nifty index starts showing signs of a significant breakout or if the options' premiums reach a predetermined profit target.

Set Position Sizing Rules: Determine how much of your trading capital you will allocate to each trade. Position sizing should align with your risk tolerance and the specific risk-reward profile of each trade.

Example: With a trading capital of INR 2,00,000, the trader will allocate 2% of their capital to each Nifty or Bank Nifty options trade, which means they will risk INR 4,000 on each trade.

Implement Risk Management: Develop a risk management strategy to protect your trading capital. This strategy should include setting stop-loss orders for each trade to limit potential losses and avoid letting losing trades run unchecked.

Example: To protect against significant losses, the trader will set a stop-loss level at 25% of the premium paid for the long straddle options and 20% of the premium received for the short strangle options. If the options' premiums reach these levels, the trader will exit the trade.

Choose Underlying Assets (Nifty and Bank Nifty): Decide on the underlying assets you will trade options on. This could be individual stocks, stock market indices, exchange-traded funds (ETFs), or other financial instruments that offer liquid options.

Example: The trader will primarily focus on trading options on the Nifty 50 index and the Bank Nifty index. Both are highly liquid and actively traded in the Indian derivatives market, providing ample trading opportunities.

Backtest Your Strategies: Before executing your trading plan in live markets, consider backtesting your strategies using historical data. Backtesting helps evaluate the effectiveness of your chosen strategies and provides insights into their performance in different market conditions.

Example: The trader will use historical data to backtest their long straddle and short strangle strategies on Nifty and Bank Nifty options. They will analyze past performance to determine the strategies' effectiveness in different market conditions and assess the risk-reward ratios in Indian rupees.

Develop Trading Rules: Establish specific trading rules that guide your actions in the market. These rules may cover aspects such as trade execution, order placement, trade management, and position adjustments.

Example: The trader will only execute trades when the entry criteria for the long straddle and short strangle strategies are met based on technical analysis and event calendars. They will place limit orders to enter and exit positions to ensure they achieve their desired prices in Indian rupees.

Review and Refine: Regularly review and refine your trading plan based on your performance and market conditions. Markets evolve, and your trading plan should be adaptable to changing circumstances.

Example: After six months of trading, the trader reviews their performance and finds that the long straddle strategy worked well during major corporate earnings releases, while the short strangle strategy performed better during sideways markets. They decide to refine their trading plan by focusing on events that historically trigger high volatility and adjust their short strangle strategy to different market conditions.

Keep a Trading Journal: Maintain a trading journal to record all your trades, including the rationale behind each trade and the outcomes. This journal helps track your progress, identify patterns, and learn from both successes and mistakes.

Example: The trader maintains a detailed trading journal, recording each Nifty and Bank Nifty options trade's specifics, including entry and exit points, profit or loss in Indian rupees, reasons for entering the trade, and market conditions at the time of the trade. This journal helps the trader identify patterns and continuously improve their trading approach.

Stay Disciplined: Once your trading plan is in place, commit to sticking to it with discipline. Avoid impulsive decisions and emotional trading by following your predefined rules and strategies.

Example: The trader follows their trading plan with discipline and avoids making impulsive decisions based on emotions. They stick to their predefined rules for trade execution, position sizing, and risk management in Indian rupees, regardless of short-term market fluctuations.

In conclusion, developing a trading plan for option trading in Nifty and Bank Nifty involves defining clear objectives, assessing risk tolerance, choosing suitable strategies, and implementing risk management techniques in Indian rupees. The plan should be based on thorough analysis, backtesting, and continuous review and refinement to adapt to changing market conditions in the Indian derivatives market. A well-structured trading plan increases a trader's chances of success and helps achieve consistent capital growth in Indian rupees over time.

## 11.5 Mindfulness and Mental Well-being:

In option trading, as in any other form of financial speculation, the emotional and psychological well-being of traders plays a crucial role in their overall success. The constant volatility, risk, and uncertainty in the financial markets can take a toll on a trader's mental health. Mindfulness is a powerful practice that can help traders manage stress, reduce emotional reactivity, and enhance their decision-making capabilities. Let's explore how mindfulness can contribute to mental well-being in option trading:

Cultivating Awareness: Mindfulness involves being fully present and aware of the present moment, without judgment or attachment to thoughts or emotions. By practicing mindfulness, traders can become more attuned to their emotions and thought patterns as they arise during trading. This self-awareness allows them to recognize and manage emotions more effectively, reducing impulsive and emotionally-driven trading decisions.

Reducing Stress and Anxiety: The financial markets can be highly stressful, especially during volatile periods or times of significant events. Mindfulness techniques, such as meditation and deep breathing exercises, have been shown to reduce stress and anxiety levels. Regular mindfulness practice can help traders remain calm and composed even in high-pressure situations, improving their ability to make rational decisions.

Improving Focus and Concentration: Mindfulness training enhances one's ability to focus and maintain concentration on the task at hand. For traders, maintaining focus during market analysis and trade execution is vital. A clear and focused mind helps traders identify trading opportunities and stay disciplined in following their trading plan.

Embracing Uncertainty: The nature of option trading involves dealing with uncertainty and unpredictability. Mindfulness encourages acceptance and non-resistance to the inevitable uncertainties in the markets. Traders who practice mindfulness are better equipped to handle losses and drawdowns with equanimity, reducing emotional distress.

Managing Impulses and Emotions: Emotions like fear and greed can influence trading decisions. Mindfulness enables traders to observe these emotions without reacting impulsively to them. Traders who practice mindfulness can pause and consider the implications of their actions before making trading decisions, leading to more rational choices.

Enhancing Mental Resilience: The ability to bounce back from setbacks is crucial in trading. Mindfulness fosters mental resilience, helping traders navigate through challenging times without losing focus or motivation. This resilience is essential for long-term success in the face of inevitable market fluctuations.

Creating Work-Life Balance: Trading can be all-consuming, leading to burnout and strain on personal relationships. Mindfulness encourages a healthy work-life balance, allowing traders to engage in self-care activities and spend time away from the screens. This balance contributes to better mental well-being and sustained trading performance.

Developing Patience: Mindfulness promotes patience by encouraging a non-reactive and non-judgmental attitude. In trading, patience is essential when waiting for the right trading opportunities and enduring drawdowns. Patient traders are more likely to stick to their trading plan and avoid impulsive decisions.

To incorporate mindfulness into their trading routine, traders can allocate a few minutes each day for meditation or mindfulness exercises. These practices can be particularly beneficial before and after trading sessions to prepare the mind for the challenges of the market and to reflect on the trading day. Additionally, traders can attend mindfulness workshops, read books on the subject, or use mindfulness apps for guidance.

In conclusion, mindfulness is a valuable tool for option traders to enhance their mental well-being and improve their trading performance. By developing self-awareness, managing stress, improving focus, and cultivating resilience, traders can navigate the markets with greater calmness, discipline, and clarity of mind. Mindfulness is not a quick fix, but with consistent practice, it can contribute to the long-term success and overall well-being of option traders.

<u>11.6 Managing Fear and Greed in Options Trading</u>

Managing fear and greed is essential for successful options trading. Fear and greed are powerful emotions that can cloud judgment and lead to impulsive decisions, often resulting in losses. Option traders need to develop strategies to control and mitigate these emotions. Here are some techniques to manage fear and greed effectively:

Set Clear Goals and Stick to a Trading Plan: Establishing clear trading goals and having a well-defined trading plan can help combat fear and greed. Traders should identify their risk tolerance, profit targets, and risk management rules. By following a structured plan, traders can avoid making emotional decisions based on fear of missing out (FOMO) or the desire for excessive profits.

Practice Risk Management: Implementing proper risk management techniques is crucial in managing fear. Setting stop-loss orders and position sizing based on risk tolerance ensures that traders don't risk more than they can afford to lose. By controlling potential losses, traders can reduce fear and emotional stress during market fluctuations.

Focus on Process, Not Outcomes: Traders should focus on executing their trading plan correctly rather than obsessing over individual trade outcomes. Fear often arises from the fear of losing money, while greed is driven by the desire for big profits. By concentrating on their trading process and adhering to their plan, traders can reduce emotional attachments to outcomes.

Avoid Overtrading: Overtrading is a common result of greed, where traders make excessive trades to capitalize on every market movement. This behavior often leads to increased risk and reduced performance. Traders should stick to their plan and avoid chasing trades out of greed.

Practice Mindfulness and Self-Awareness: Mindfulness techniques can help traders become more self-aware of their emotions and thought patterns. By acknowledging fear and greed as they arise, traders can prevent these emotions from influencing their trading decisions. Techniques such as deep breathing or taking breaks during trading sessions can help manage emotional responses.

Learn from Past Mistakes: Fear and greed often stem from past experiences. Traders should review and analyze their previous trades to identify patterns of emotional decision-making. By learning from past mistakes, traders can improve their decision-making process and avoid repeating errors driven by fear or greed.

Set Realistic Expectations: Managing greed involves setting realistic expectations for trading returns. It's essential to understand that consistent profitability takes time and effort. Unrealistic profit targets can lead to impulsive and risky trades, driven by greed.

Stay Informed and Educated: Fear can arise from uncertainty and lack of knowledge. To combat this, traders should stay informed about the markets and continuously educate themselves about options trading strategies. Knowledge and preparation can instill confidence and reduce fear.

Take Breaks and Seek Support: Emotional strain from fear and greed can take a toll on traders. Taking breaks from the market and engaging in other activities can help alleviate stress. Additionally, seeking support from fellow traders, mentors, or trading communities can provide valuable insights and encouragement during challenging times.

By proactively addressing fear and greed, option traders can improve their decision-making process and maintain a disciplined approach to trading. Managing these emotions is an ongoing practice, and with time, traders can develop greater emotional intelligence and improve their overall trading performance.

11.7 Visualization and Goal Setting:

Visualization and goal setting are powerful techniques that can significantly impact a trader's success in option trading. By setting clear and achievable goals and using visualization to reinforce positive outcomes, traders can enhance their focus, motivation, and overall performance. Here's how visualization and goal setting can be effectively used in option trading:

Goal Setting: Define Specific and Measurable Goals: Clearly define what you want to achieve through option trading. Goals should be specific, measurable, achievable, relevant, and time-bound (SMART). For example, setting a goal to achieve a 15% return on investment in Nifty options over six months.

Break Goals into Milestones: Break down larger goals into smaller milestones to track progress and stay motivated. These milestones can serve as checkpoints to assess if you are on track to achieve your main objectives.

Set Realistic Expectations: While it's essential to challenge yourself, set goals that are realistic and attainable based on your trading experience, capital, and risk tolerance. Unrealistic goals can lead to frustration and negatively impact trading decisions.

Write Down Your Goals: Document your goals in writing, as this helps solidify your commitment to them. Having written goals also allows you to review and revise them periodically as your trading journey progresses.

Visualization: Create Mental Images of Success: Visualization involves creating vivid mental images of successfully achieving your trading goals. Imagine yourself executing profitable trades, sticking to your trading plan, and handling emotions calmly during market fluctuations.

Engage All Your Senses: Make your visualizations as detailed as possible by engaging all your senses. Feel the excitement of making profitable trades, see the charts moving in your favor, and hear the sounds of a successful trade execution.

Visualize Overcoming Challenges: In addition to positive outcomes, visualize yourself effectively dealing with challenges and setbacks. This will help build mental resilience and prepare you for adverse market conditions.

Practice Regularly: Set aside time daily or before trading sessions to practice visualization. Consistency is key to making visualization a powerful habit that influences your mindset positively.

Combining Visualization and Goal Setting: Visualize Your Goal Achievement: Before setting out to achieve your trading goals, spend time visualizing yourself successfully accomplishing them. This mental rehearsal can boost your confidence and reinforce your commitment to reaching those goals.

Align Visualization with Your Trading Plan: Visualize the specific actions and decisions you need to take to achieve your goals, in line with your trading plan. See yourself adhering to your entry and exit criteria, managing risk, and staying disciplined.

Review Progress Regularly: As you progress toward your trading goals, regularly review and update your visualizations and milestones. Celebrate your achievements and make any necessary adjustments to your goals or visualization techniques.

Use Visualization to Manage Emotions: During stressful or challenging trading moments, use visualization to calm your nerves and refocus your mind. Visualize yourself staying composed and making rational decisions.

Remember that visualization and goal setting are not a substitute for diligent market analysis and proper trading strategies. They are tools to enhance your trading mindset and motivation. By setting clear, achievable goals and using visualization to reinforce positive outcomes, option traders can develop a focused and disciplined approach, leading to improved performance and increased chances of success in the markets.

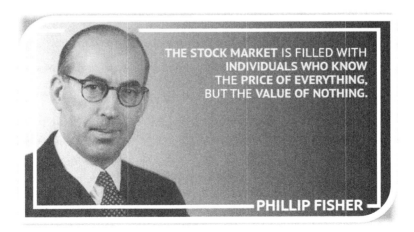

THE STOCK MARKET IS FILLED WITH INDIVIDUALS WHO KNOW THE PRICE OF EVERYTHING, BUT THE VALUE OF NOTHING.

PHILLIP FISHER

## Chapter 12: Building a Trading System and Strategy

12.1 Defining Your Trading Style and Goals:

Before building a trading system and strategy for Indian share market Nifty and Bank Nifty, it's essential to define your trading style and goals. Your trading style will determine the frequency of your trades, the holding period of positions, and the strategies you'll use. Your trading goals will outline what you aim to achieve through trading, such as capital growth, income generation, or risk management. Let's explore this in more detail with Indian market examples:

Trading Style:

a. Day Trading: Day traders buy and sell financial instruments within the same trading day, aiming to profit from short-term price movements. They don't hold positions overnight, reducing the exposure to overnight market risks.

Example for Indian Market: A day trader in the Indian market may focus on trading liquid stocks like Reliance Industries (RELIANCE) or Tata Consultancy Services (TCS) using technical indicators and intra-day price patterns.

b. Swing Trading: Swing traders hold positions for several days to a few weeks, seeking to profit from price swings within a broader trend. Swing trading allows traders to capture medium-term price movements.

Example for Indian Market: A swing trader in the Indian market may trade Nifty and Bank Nifty futures, looking for opportunities based on chart patterns and technical indicators like moving averages.

c. Position Trading: Position traders hold positions for an extended period, ranging from weeks to months, based on long-term fundamental analysis and macroeconomic trends.

Example for Indian Market: A position trader in the Indian market may invest in blue-chip stocks like HDFC Bank or Infosys, taking a long-term view on India's economic growth and specific sector trends.

Trading Goals:

a. Capital Growth: The primary goal of many traders is to achieve consistent capital growth. This involves increasing the value of their trading account over time through profitable trading activities.

Example: A day trader in the Indian market may aim to achieve a 10% return on their trading capital every month by taking advantage of intra-day price movements.

b. Risk Management: Some traders prioritize risk management and capital preservation over aggressive profit targets. Their goal is to protect their trading capital from substantial losses.

Example: A swing trader in the Indian market may focus on maintaining a maximum drawdown of 5% on their trading capital to ensure risk is well-controlled.

c. Income Generation: Income-focused traders seek to generate regular income from their trading activities, supplementing their existing earnings.

Example: A position trader in the Indian market may focus on dividend-paying stocks like Hindustan Unilever (HINDUNILVR) to earn a steady stream of dividends.

d. Portfolio Diversification: Some traders use trading to diversify their overall investment portfolio, reducing their exposure to specific market risks.

Example: A swing trader in the Indian market may allocate a portion of their investment capital to trading commodities like gold or silver to diversify their portfolio.

Defining your trading style and goals in the Indian market is crucial for developing a trading system that aligns with your objectives. Whether you prefer day trading, swing trading, or position trading, and whether your goals are capital growth, risk management, income generation, or portfolio diversification, your trading system should be designed to suit your unique preferences and objectives. Always remember that successful trading requires discipline, proper risk management, and continuous evaluation and improvement of your strategies.

12.2 Components of a Trading System

Building a trading system requires the integration of various components that work together to guide a trader's decision-making process. Each component plays a crucial role in the overall effectiveness of the system. Let's delve into the key components of a trading system:

Entry and Exit Signals:

Entry and exit signals are specific conditions or criteria that trigger a trade. These signals are based on technical analysis, fundamental analysis, or a combination of both. The goal is to identify optimal entry points to initiate a trade and exit points to lock in profits or cut losses.

Example: For a swing trading system in the Indian market, a common entry signal could be when the 50-day moving average crosses above the 200-day moving average, indicating a potential bullish trend. An exit signal may be triggered when the price crosses below the 20-day moving average.

Risk Management Rules:

Risk management rules are essential for protecting trading capital and preventing significant losses. They determine how much capital to risk on each trade and where to set stop-loss orders to limit potential losses.

Example: In the Indian market, a trader may decide to risk only 1% of their trading capital on any single trade. They will place a stop-loss order at a certain price level to exit the trade if it moves against them beyond a specified point.

Position Sizing:

Position sizing refers to determining the number of shares, contracts, or lots to trade based on the level of risk defined by the risk management rules. Proper position sizing ensures that each trade carries a consistent level of risk.

Example: If a trader's risk management rule is to risk 2% of their trading capital per trade and their stop-loss is set at INR 10 per share, they will calculate the position size such that the total potential loss does not exceed 2% of their capital.

Trade Filters:

Trade filters are additional criteria used to filter out potential trades that do not meet specific conditions. These filters help traders focus on high-probability trades and avoid entering low-quality setups.

Example: A trader may use trade filters such as volatility levels, specific chart patterns, or macroeconomic indicators to confirm the validity of their entry and exit signals before executing a trade.

Trade Management Techniques:

Trade management techniques refer to the methods used to manage a trade once it's open. This includes trailing stops, partial profit-taking, or adjusting stop-loss levels based on market conditions.

Example: A trader may use a trailing stop to lock in profits as the trade moves in their favor. If the trade reaches a certain profit target, they may decide to take partial profits and adjust the stop-loss to break-even to reduce risk.

Backtesting and Historical Data Analysis:

Backtesting involves testing the trading system on historical market data to assess its performance. This process helps traders identify potential strengths and weaknesses in the system and refine their strategies.

Example: Traders can use historical price data for the Indian market to backtest their trading system over a specific period and analyze metrics such as win rate, average profit, and drawdown.

In conclusion, a robust trading system should incorporate well-defined entry and exit signals, risk management rules, position sizing, trade filters, trade management techniques, and a thorough backtesting process. Each component is essential for creating a systematic and disciplined approach to trading, increasing the probability of success in the dynamic and competitive financial markets.

## 12.3 Strategy Development and Testing

Strategy development and testing are crucial steps in building a successful trading system. Developing a well-defined trading strategy involves formulating specific rules for entry, exit, risk management, and position sizing. After the strategy is developed, it needs to be tested on historical data to assess its performance and viability. Let's explore these steps in detail:

Strategy Development:

a. Entry Rules: Define clear and objective conditions that signal when to enter a trade. Entry rules can be based on technical indicators, chart patterns, fundamental analysis, or a combination of factors.

Example: A swing trading strategy for the Indian market may have an entry rule to buy a particular stock when its 20-day moving average crosses above its 50-day moving average.

b. Exit Rules: Establish rules that determine when to exit a trade to lock in profits or cut losses. Exit rules should be based on price targets, technical signals, or trailing stops.

Example: The same swing trading strategy may have an exit rule to sell the stock if it reaches a certain percentage profit or if the price falls below the 20-day moving average.

c. Risk Management: Set rules for managing risk in each trade. This includes determining the maximum percentage of capital to risk per trade and where to place stop-loss orders.

Example: The strategy may have a risk management rule to risk only 2% of the trading capital on each trade and set the stop-loss at a specific percentage below the entry price.

d. Position Sizing: Determine how much of the trading capital to allocate to each trade. Position sizing ensures that the risk per trade is consistent with the risk management rules.

Example: Based on the risk management rule of 2% per trade and the stop-loss level, the strategy will calculate the position size to ensure that the total potential loss is limited to 2% of the trading capital.

Backtesting and Testing:

a. Historical Data: Obtain historical price data for the relevant financial instruments to be traded, such as stocks, commodities, or indices in the Indian market.

b. Backtesting: Apply the strategy rules to the historical data to simulate past trades. This process helps assess the strategy's performance, including the number of winning and losing trades, average profit, drawdowns, and risk-reward ratios.

c. Optimization: After backtesting, traders may consider optimizing the strategy by adjusting parameters to improve its performance. However, it's essential to avoid overfitting or curve-fitting the strategy to historical data.

d. Forward Testing: Implement the strategy in real-time with small position sizes or on a demo account to observe its performance in current market conditions.

e. Walk-Forward Testing: Continuously assess and refine the strategy as new market data becomes available. This process helps ensure the strategy remains effective in changing market conditions.

Evaluation and Refinement:

Based on the backtesting and forward testing results, evaluate the strategy's performance and identify areas for improvement. Traders may refine the strategy by adjusting entry or exit rules, risk management, or position sizing as needed.

Regularly monitor the strategy's performance in live markets and keep a trading journal to record trade details and notes on improvements. This iterative process helps develop a robust and adaptive trading strategy.

In conclusion, strategy development and testing are vital components of building a successful trading system. By formulating clear and objective rules for entry, exit, risk management, and position sizing, and rigorously testing the strategy on historical and real-time data, traders can develop a systematic and disciplined approach to trading that improves the probability of success in the Indian market or any other financial market.

12.4 Optimization and Parameter Selection:

Optimization and parameter selection are important steps in refining a trading strategy to improve its performance. However, it's essential to approach optimization cautiously to avoid overfitting the strategy to historical data. Let's explore how optimization and parameter selection can be effectively done:

Understanding Optimization:

Optimization involves adjusting specific parameters or variables within the trading strategy to maximize its performance metrics, such as profitability or risk-adjusted returns. Parameters that can be optimized include moving average periods, RSI thresholds, stop-loss levels, and profit targets, among others.

Selecting Performance Metrics:

Before optimizing the strategy, it's crucial to identify the performance metrics that matter the most to you. Common metrics include:

Net Profit: The total profit generated by the strategy over a specific period.

Win Rate: The percentage of winning trades out of total trades.

Average Profit per Trade: The average profit generated per trade.

Maximum Drawdown: The maximum percentage decline from the strategy's peak value.

Setting Optimization Constraints:

To prevent overfitting, traders should set constraints during the optimization process. Constraints limit the range of parameter values that can be tested and prevent the strategy from being overly optimized for historical data.

Using Different Time Periods:

To verify the robustness of the optimized strategy, it's essential to test it on different time periods and market conditions. This process is known as walk-forward testing, where the strategy is optimized on a specific historical period and then tested on a subsequent period.

Considering Out-of-Sample Testing:

Out-of-sample testing involves using a portion of the historical data that was not used during the optimization process to validate the strategy's performance. This helps assess the strategy's ability to perform well on unseen data.

Avoiding Over-Optimization:

Over-optimization occurs when a strategy is excessively tailored to historical data, making it less effective in real-time trading. To avoid overfitting, consider using simpler and more robust parameter values.

Focus on Stability and Consistency:

Instead of pursuing the highest possible performance metrics, focus on stability and consistency in the strategy's results. A stable and consistent strategy is more likely to perform well in different market conditions.

Relying on Your Judgment:

While optimization tools can assist in refining a strategy, traders should not solely rely on automated optimization results. Their judgment and understanding of the market should play a significant role in selecting the final parameters.

In conclusion, optimization and parameter selection are valuable tools to improve the performance of a trading strategy. By selecting appropriate performance metrics, setting optimization constraints, performing out-of-sample testing, and avoiding over-optimization, traders can refine their strategies to be more robust and adaptive to changing market conditions. The key is to strike a balance between performance and stability, ensuring that the strategy remains effective over the long term.

## 12.5 System Monitoring and Evaluation:

System monitoring and evaluation are essential ongoing processes to ensure the trading system remains effective and aligned with market conditions. Regularly monitoring and evaluating the performance of the trading system allows traders to identify strengths, weaknesses, and areas for improvement. Let's explore the key steps involved in system monitoring and evaluation:

Keep a Trading Journal:

Maintain a detailed trading journal where you record all your trades, including entry and exit points, trade rationale, position sizing, risk management, and any notes about the trade's outcome. A trading journal helps you track your progress, learn from your experiences, and make data-driven decisions.

Review Trade Performance:

Regularly review the performance of individual trades and the overall trading system. Assess the profitability, win rate, average profit per trade, maximum drawdown, and other relevant metrics. Identify patterns and trends in your trading results to understand what is working and what needs improvement.

Analyse Trading Psychology:

Evaluate your emotional state during trades and assess how emotions such as fear, greed, or overconfidence may have influenced your decisions. Identifying patterns of emotional behavior can help you address psychological biases and improve your decision-making process.

Track Market Conditions:

Monitor the prevailing market conditions during your trades. Note how the system performs in different market environments, such as trending, ranging, or volatile markets. This analysis can help you adjust the system to perform better under specific conditions.

Conduct Walk-Forward Testing:

Perform walk-forward testing, where you periodically re-optimize the trading system using new data and validate its performance on subsequent periods. This process ensures that the system remains adaptive to changing market conditions.

Regularly Update the System:

As you gain more insights from monitoring and evaluation, update your trading system accordingly. This may involve fine-tuning entry and exit rules, adjusting risk management parameters, or incorporating new filters based on your observations.

Set Realistic Expectations:

Maintain realistic expectations about the trading system's performance. Avoid making hasty decisions based on short-term results. Trading performance can vary over time, and it's essential to stick to a systematic approach and remain disciplined.

Seek External Feedback:

Discuss your trading system and results with other traders or mentors to gain valuable external perspectives. Feedback from experienced traders can help you identify blind spots and offer constructive suggestions for improvement.

Be Patient and Adaptive:

Evaluate your trading system over a meaningful period, typically several months or more, to gather sufficient data. Be patient and avoid making frequent changes based on short-term fluctuations. Allow the system to adapt and improve over time.

Stay Informed and Educated:

Keep up-to-date with market developments, new trading strategies, and changes in market conditions. Continuous learning and staying informed can help you enhance your trading system and overall trading performance.

In conclusion, system monitoring and evaluation are ongoing processes that enable traders to fine-tune and optimize their trading systems based on real-world data and market conditions. Regularly analyzing trade performance, tracking market conditions, and learning from experiences are crucial for continuous improvement and long-term success in trading. A systematic and disciplined approach to monitoring and evaluating the trading system contributes to improved decision-making and ultimately better trading outcomes.

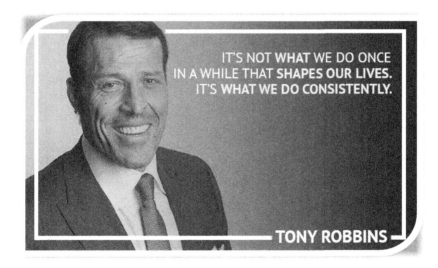

## Chapter 13: Backtesting and Paper Trading

13.1 Importance of Backtesting:

Backtesting is a crucial process that allows traders to evaluate the performance of a trading strategy using historical data. It helps traders assess how well the strategy would have performed in past market conditions before risking real capital. The importance of backtesting lies in the following aspects:

a. Performance Evaluation: Backtesting provides objective data on the strategy's historical performance, including win rate, average profit, drawdown, and risk-reward ratio.

b. Strategy Validation: By backtesting, traders can validate whether their trading strategy has an edge in the markets and if it aligns with their trading goals.

c. Risk Reduction: Backtesting helps identify potential flaws and weaknesses in the strategy, allowing traders to make improvements and reduce the risk of substantial losses.

d. Confidence Building: Positive backtesting results instill confidence in traders, reinforcing their belief in the trading system and increasing their commitment to follow it consistently.

13.2 Creating a Backtesting Plan:

To conduct effective backtesting, traders should follow a structured plan:

a. Define Strategy Rules: Clearly define the entry, exit, and risk management rules of the trading strategy, including technical indicators and parameters.

b. Select Historical Data: Choose a relevant period of historical data for backtesting, ideally including different market conditions.

c. Set Trading Parameters: Decide on the position size, commission, slippage, and other trading costs to reflect real-world conditions accurately.

d. Perform Backtesting: Implement the strategy on historical data, following the defined rules, and record all trade details.

e. Analyze Results: Evaluate the backtesting results to understand the strategy's performance and draw insights for improvements.

## 13.3 Paper Trading Strategies:

Paper trading, also known as simulated trading or virtual trading, involves executing trades on paper or using a trading simulator without risking real money. It allows traders to practice and validate their strategies in real-time market conditions without the fear of financial loss. The key benefits of paper trading are:

a. Skill Development: Paper trading helps traders gain experience, refine their strategies, and build confidence before transitioning to live trading.

b. Risk-Free Learning: Traders can experiment with different ideas and approaches without risking their capital.

c. Error Identification: Paper trading helps identify potential flaws or inefficiencies in the strategy, enabling traders to make necessary adjustments.

d. Market Familiarization: Traders get familiar with order types, execution speed, and platform functionalities.

## 13.4 Analyzing Backtesting Results:

Analyzing backtesting results is a crucial step to understand the strategy's performance and identify areas for improvement:

a. Performance Metrics: Review metrics like win rate, average profit, maximum drawdown, and risk-reward ratio to assess the strategy's effectiveness.

b. Market Conditions: Observe how the strategy performs in different market conditions, such as trending, ranging, or volatile markets.

c. Robustness: Evaluate if the strategy remains effective over multiple time periods and different market environments.

d. Error Identification: Identify any discrepancies between the backtesting results and the expected outcomes based on the strategy's rules.

13.5 Incorporating Backtesting into Your Trading Routine:

To make the most of backtesting, traders should integrate it into their regular trading routine:

a. Continuous Improvement: Regularly backtest and refine your trading strategies to adapt to changing market conditions.

b. Validation: Before implementing a new strategy, thoroughly backtest it to validate its performance and gain confidence in its potential.

c. Walk-Forward Testing: After optimization, perform walk-forward testing to validate the strategy's performance on new data.

d. Realistic Expectations: Set realistic expectations based on backtesting results and avoid over-optimizing the strategy for historical data.

Incorporating back testing into your trading routine can significantly enhance your trading decisions, improve performance, and build a systematic and disciplined approach to the Indian shares market or any other financial market.

IF YOU CAN **LEARN TO CREATE A STATE OF MIND THAT IS NOT AFFECTED BY THE MARKET'S BEHAVIOUR,** THE STRUGGLE WILL CEASE TO EXIST.

— MARK DOUGLAS

## Chapter 14: Tips for Successful Options Trading in India

14.1 The Importance of Discipline and Patience:

Discipline and patience are essential traits for successful options trading in the Indian market. Here's why they matter and how to incorporate them into your trading approach:

a. Stick to Your Trading Plan: Develop a well-defined trading plan with clear entry and exit rules, risk management strategies, and position sizing. Adhere to your plan consistently, avoiding impulsive decisions based on emotions or market noise.

b. Avoid Overtrading: Resist the temptation to trade excessively, as it can lead to increased transaction costs and dilute your focus on high-quality setups. Wait for opportunities that align with your trading strategy.

c. Manage Risk: Prioritize risk management by setting appropriate stop-loss levels and position sizes. Avoid taking excessive risks that could jeopardize your trading capital.

d. Exercise Patience: Be patient and wait for the right trading opportunities to come along. Don't force trades or chase market movements.

14.2 Avoiding Common Mistakes in Options Trading:

Avoiding common mistakes can significantly improve your options trading performance. Here are some mistakes to watch out for:

a. Neglecting Risk Management: Failing to implement proper risk management can lead to substantial losses. Always define your risk per trade and set stop-loss levels accordingly.

b. Overlooking Liquidity: Trade liquid options with sufficient trading volume to ensure smooth entry and exit without slippage.

c. Ignoring Implied Volatility: Understand the impact of implied volatility on option prices. Avoid buying options when implied volatility is high, as it can lead to expensive premiums.

d. Not Diversifying: Diversify your options trades across different assets and strategies to spread risk and reduce the impact of adverse market moves.

## 14.3 Keeping Up with Market Trends and News:

Staying informed about market trends and news is crucial for making informed trading decisions:

a. Economic Calendar: Keep track of major economic events, corporate earnings releases, and policy decisions that can influence market sentiment.

b. Technical Analysis: Use technical analysis tools to identify trends, support and resistance levels, and potential entry and exit points.

c. Sector Analysis: Monitor specific sectors and industries that may have a significant impact on the performance of underlying assets.

d. Option Greeks: Understand and analyze option Greeks, such as Delta, Gamma, Theta, Vega, and Rho, to assess the sensitivity of options to different factors.

## 14.4 The Role of Emotions in Trading:

Controlling emotions is vital in options trading to make rational and objective decisions:

a. Avoid Fear and Greed: Fear and greed can cloud judgment and lead to impulsive decisions. Stick to your trading plan and avoid emotional trading.

b. Maintain Emotional Balance: Develop strategies to manage stress and emotions during market fluctuations. Take breaks, practice mindfulness, or engage in stress-relieving activities.

c. Learn from Mistakes: Analyze your trading mistakes objectively and use them as learning opportunities to improve your future decisions.

d. Stay Detached from Outcomes: Focus on executing your trading plan and don't get emotionally attached to individual trades' outcomes.

In conclusion, successful options trading in the Indian market requires discipline, patience, risk management, and the ability to control emotions. By avoiding common mistakes, staying informed about market trends, and maintaining emotional balance, traders can improve their chances of success and achieve consistent results in their options trading endeavors.

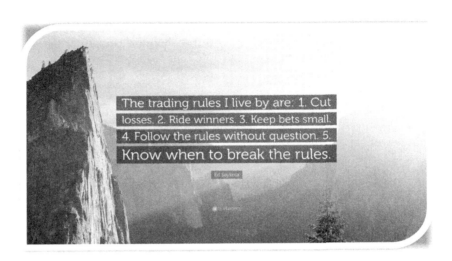

The trading rules I live by are: 1. Cut losses. 2. Ride winners. 3. Keep bets small. 4. Follow the rules without question. 5. Know when to break the rules.

Ed Seykota

# Chapter 15: The Future of Options Trading in India

## 15.1 Evolving Market Trends:

Options trading in India is expected to witness several evolving trends in the future. These trends will be influenced by changes in market dynamics, investor preferences, regulatory developments, and global economic factors. Some of the key evolving market trends in options trading in India are:

a. Increased Retail Participation: As awareness about options trading grows and online trading platforms become more accessible, retail investors are likely to participate more actively in the options market.

b. Algorithmic Trading: Algorithmic and high-frequency trading are expected to gain prominence in the options market, driven by advancements in technology and the need for faster execution and efficient risk management.

c. Introduction of New Products: Exchanges may introduce innovative option products to cater to diverse investor needs and hedging requirements, such as sector-specific options, volatility-based options, or options on new underlying assets.

d. Integration of ESG Principles: Environmental, Social, and Governance (ESG) considerations are becoming increasingly important in financial markets. Options exchanges may incorporate ESG-related options contracts to meet the demand for sustainable investing.

## 15.2 Technology and Innovation in Options Trading:

Advancements in technology will play a significant role in shaping the future of options trading in India:

a. Electronic Trading Platforms: Options trading is likely to become more electronic and automated, enabling seamless order execution and access to a broader range of participants.

b. Artificial Intelligence (AI) and Machine Learning (ML): AI and ML technologies will be increasingly used for data analysis, market predictions, and trading strategy optimization, enhancing the efficiency of options trading.

c. Blockchain and Smart Contracts: Blockchain technology can facilitate transparent and secure options trading through smart contracts, reducing counterparty risk and settlement times.

d. Mobile Trading: The growth of mobile trading apps will enable investors to trade options on the go, democratizing access to the options market.

15.3 Global Market Integration and Impact on Indian Options Trading:

An Indian option trading is likely to be influenced by global market integration and interconnectivity:

a. Cross-Border Trading: Indian investors may gain easier access to global options markets, and foreign investors may find opportunities in Indian options through cross-border trading agreements.

b. Increased Correlations: The integration of Indian financial markets with global markets may lead to increased correlations between Indian assets and global assets, impacting option pricing and risk management strategies.

c. Regulatory Harmonization: As global financial markets harmonize regulations, Indian options exchanges may adopt international best practices to align with global standards.

d. Global Events and Macro Factors: Indian options trading may become more sensitive to global events and macroeconomic factors, necessitating robust risk management strategies.

In conclusion, the future of options trading in India is likely to be shaped by evolving market trends, technological innovations, and increased global market integration. Retail participation, algorithmic trading, product diversification, and the integration of technology are expected to drive the growth of the options market. Traders and investors should remain adaptable to these changes and leverage technology to make informed decisions in the dynamic landscape of options trading in India.

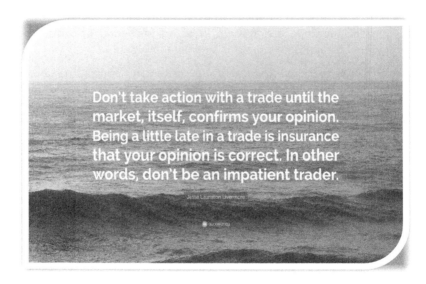

Don't take action with a trade until the market, itself, confirms your opinion. Being a little late in a trade is insurance that your opinion is correct. In other words, don't be an impatient trader.

Jesse Lauriston Livermore

## Chapter 16: Lessons Learned in Options Trading

### 16.1 Lessons Learned from Failures and Mistakes:

a. Risk Management is Paramount: One of the most critical lessons in options trading is the importance of risk management. Many traders have experienced significant losses due to inadequate risk management. Always determine the maximum amount of capital you are willing to risk on each trade (often a percentage of your total trading capital) and set stop-loss levels accordingly. This ensures that a losing trade doesn't wipe out a substantial portion of your trading account.

b. Emotional Discipline: Emotions play a significant role in trading, and failing to control them can lead to poor decision-making. Greed can cause traders to hold on to winning positions for too long, hoping for more profits, only to see the market reverse. Fear can cause traders to exit winning trades prematurely, missing out on potential gains. It's crucial to develop emotional discipline, stick to your trading plan, and avoid making impulsive decisions based on emotions.

c. Avoid Overconfidence: After a series of successful trades, traders may become overconfident in their abilities. Overconfidence can lead to taking excessive risks or deviating from proven strategies, which can result in losses. Stay humble and remember that the markets are unpredictable. Stick to your trading plan and avoid taking unnecessary risks just because you have experienced some recent successes.

d. Patience and Timing: Rushing into trades without proper analysis or waiting for the right setup can lead to poor outcomes. Patience is essential in options trading. Wait for the right trading opportunities that align with your strategy and execute them with proper timing. Avoid the temptation to enter trades just for the sake of being in the market.

### 16.2 Adapting to Changing Market Conditions:

a. Stay Informed: The financial markets are influenced by a wide range of factors, including economic data, geopolitical events, and corporate earnings reports. Stay informed about market news, economic calendars, and relevant global developments that may impact the options market. Being aware of upcoming events can help you adjust your trading strategies accordingly.

b. Flexibility in Strategies: No single trading strategy works in all market conditions. Be open to modifying or diversifying your trading strategies based on the prevailing market environment. A strategy that works well in a trending market may not perform as effectively in a range-bound or volatile market. Stay adaptable and be prepared to switch to strategies that suit the current conditions.

c. Test and Validate: Continuously test and validate your trading strategies under various market scenarios using historical data. Backtesting allows you to assess how your strategies would have performed in past market conditions. This process helps you identify strengths and weaknesses and refine your strategies for future adaptability.

d. Recognize Market Cycles: Financial markets move in cycles, shifting between trending, ranging, and volatile phases. Recognize these market cycles and adjust your trading approach accordingly. In trending markets, trend-following strategies may work well, while range-bound markets may require mean-reversion strategies.

16.3 Overcoming Challenges in Options Trading:

a. Education and Skill Development: Options trading involves complex financial instruments and various strategies. Continuous learning and skill development are essential for traders to make informed decisions. Invest time in understanding option Greeks, volatility, and various options trading strategies. Attend workshops, read books, and follow reputable financial websites and educational resources to enhance your knowledge.

b. Avoiding Overtrading: Overtrading is a common challenge faced by traders, particularly beginners. It can lead to increased transaction costs, emotional exhaustion, and dilution of focus on high-quality setups. Avoid the temptation to trade excessively. Stick to your trading plan and only execute trades that meet your predefined criteria.

c. Embracing Uncertainty: Trading involves inherent uncertainty and risk. Not all trades will be winners, and losses are a part of the process. Embrace uncertainty and avoid being emotionally attached to individual trades' outcomes. Focus on executing your trading plan and managing risk effectively. Understand that consistent profitability is achieved over time, not from any single trade.

d. Learn from Experienced Traders: Seek guidance from experienced traders or mentors who have navigated the challenges of options trading successfully. Engaging with a trading community can provide valuable insights and support. Learning from the experiences of others can help you avoid common pitfalls and accelerate your learning curve.

In conclusion, learning from failures and mistakes is an essential aspect of becoming a successful options trader. Emphasize risk management, develop emotional discipline, avoid overconfidence, and be patient in waiting for the right trading opportunities. Adapt to changing market conditions, stay informed, and validate your trading strategies through backtesting. Overcoming challenges requires continuous education, avoiding overtrading, embracing uncertainty, and seeking advice from experienced traders. By incorporating these lessons into your options trading approach, you can improve your decision-making and increase your chances of long-term success in the dynamic world of options trading.

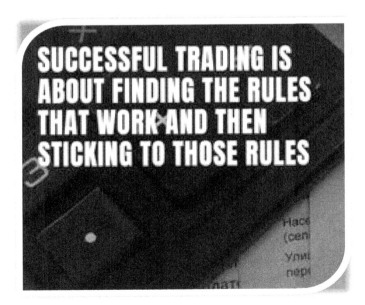

## Conclusion

In conclusion, "Mastering Options Trading in the Indian Market" provides a comprehensive and invaluable guide to navigating the complexities of options trading in the dynamic Indian financial landscape. Throughout the book, readers have been exposed to a wealth of knowledge, strategies, and real-world examples that demystify the intricacies of options trading, empowering them to make well-informed decisions and succeed in their trading endeavors.

The book begins by laying a strong foundation, offering a clear explanation of options, their various types, and the associated terminologies. It then progresses into more advanced topics, delving into different options trading strategies, including bullish, bearish, and neutral approaches, and how to select the right strategy for specific market conditions. Moreover, the book explores the concept of risk management, emphasizing its crucial role in safeguarding capital and mitigating potential losses.

A standout feature of this book is its emphasis on tailoring the content to suit the unique aspects of the Indian financial market. By understanding the nuances of the Indian stock market, readers are equipped with valuable insights that enable them to apply the strategies effectively and capitalize on local market trends.

The author's expert guidance and practical approach further enhance the book's value. By including numerous real-world examples and case studies, readers are given a glimpse into how successful traders think and operate, offering valuable lessons that can be applied to their own trading journey.

As readers progress through the book, they are encouraged to develop a disciplined and patient trading mind-set. This emphasis on a long-term perspective and continuous learning will undoubtedly contribute to their growth as successful and knowledgeable traders.

In essence, "Mastering Options Trading in the Indian Market" is a must-read for both novice and experienced traders seeking to deepen their understanding of options trading in India. The book's clarity, depth, and practicality make it an indispensable resource that will serve as a reliable companion on the path to trading mastery. As readers embrace the principles outlined in this book and apply them diligently, they are well-positioned to navigate the complexities of the Indian market with confidence, resilience, and profitability.

**Notes:**

Printed in Great Britain
by Amazon

43814696R00066